THE READER'S DIGEST
Children's Book of

The Human Body

THE READER'S DIGEST
Children's Book of
The Human Body

A Reader's Digest® Children's Book,
published 1999 by Reader's Digest Children's Publishing Ltd,
King's Court, Parsonage Lane, Bath BA1 1ER,
a subsidiary of The Reader's Digest Association, Inc.

Conceived and produced by Weldon Owen Pty Limited
59 Victoria Street, McMahons Point, NSW, 2060, Australia
A member of the Weldon Owen Group of Companies
Sydney • San Francisco

© Weldon Owen Inc., 1999

READER'S DIGEST CHILDREN'S BOOKS
General Manager: Vivian Antonangeli
Group Publisher: Rosanna Hansen
Managing Editor: Cathy Jones
Editor: Louise Pritchard
Assistant Editor: Sarah Williams

WELDON OWEN PTY LTD
Chairman: John Owen
Publisher: Sheena Coupe
Associate Publisher: Lynn Humphries
Art Director: Sue Burk
Consultant, Design Concept and Cover Design: John Bull
Design Concept: Clare Forte, Robyn Latimer
Editorial Assistants: Sarah Anderson, Trudie Craig
Production Manager: Caroline Webber
Production Assistant: Kylie Lawson
Vice President International Sales: Stuart Laurence

Author: Laurie Beckelman
Consultant: Jonathan Stein, M.D.
Project Editor: Klay Lamprell
Designers: Cliff Burk, Robyn Latimer, Sue Rawkins
DTP: Rebecca Kocass/Hocass Pocass Design
Picture Research: Annette Crueger

Illustrators: Susanna Addario, Marcus Cremonese, Sam & Amy Collins,
Christer Eriksson, Peg Gerrity, Gino Hasler, Jeff Lang, Siri Mills, Spencer Phippen,
Kate Sweeney/K.E. Sweeney Illustration, Rod Westblade

British Library Cataloguing in Publication Data.
A catalogue record for this book is available
from the British Library.

Colour Reproduction by Colourscan Co Pte Ltd
Printed by Tien Wah Press Pte Ltd
Printed in Singapore

A WELDON OWEN PRODUCTION

THE READER'S DIGEST
Children's Book of

The Human Body

A Reader's Digest Children's Book

Contents

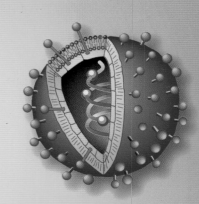

Control Centres   6

The Framework   32

Supplies and Demand   46

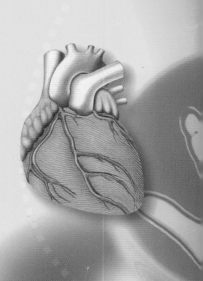

Pick Your Path!

PREPARE YOURSELF FOR a journey through *The Human Body* like no other. You can read straight through to the end to discover what we now know about our amazing bodies – and what we might learn in the future. Or, if you want to find out more about a subject, use the 'Pathfinder'.

You'll find plenty of other paths to choose from in the special features sections. Read about the heroes of human biology in 'Inside Story', or get creative with 'Hands On' activities. Delve into words with 'Word Builders', or amaze your friends with fascinating facts from 'That's Amazing!' You can choose a new path with every reading – THE READER'S DIGEST CHILDREN'S BOOK OF THE HUMAN BODY will take you wherever *you* want to go.

INSIDE STORY

Heroes of Science

Picture yourself alongside a doctor who dips food into an open stomach wound to learn more about digestion. Share a scientist's excitement as he discovers X-rays. Learn why a child with diabetes must give herself an injection each day. Explore life in the womb. INSIDE STORY introduces you to the men and women behind the science, and gives you an insider's look at new tools and treatments. Read about them and make yourself a part of the discoveries that have changed the world.

HANDS ON

Things to Do

Trick your brain into seeing a hole in your hand. Use buckets of water to understand how much blood the heart pumps each day. Assemble straws and cardboard into a 'bone' and test it for strength. Find out how long it takes for a yawn to catch on. The HANDS ON features suggest experiments, projects, and activities that demonstrate how the body works.

Word Builders

What a strange word! What does it mean? Where did it come from? Find out by reading **Word Builders**.

That's Amazing!

Astounding facts, amazing records, fascinating figures – you'll find them all in **That's Amazing!**

Pathfinder

Use the **Pathfinder** section to find your way from one subject to another. It's all up to you.

Ready! Steady! Start exploring!

Control Centres

YOUR BODY IS a familiar friend. You know it so well that you probably don't think about it much. But beneath your freckles, dimples or knobby knees is a world as vast as the universe. Millions of cells work together so you can breathe, move, eat, think, talk and grow. How does your amazing body make this teamwork possible? You're about to find out.

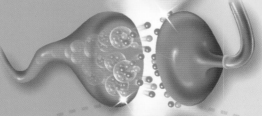

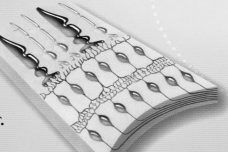
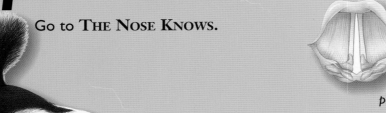

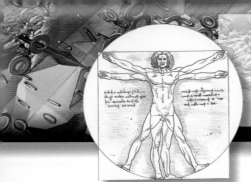

Amazing Us

HAVE YOU WONDERED how you grow, why you get ill or why people die? If so, you share a curiosity as old as humankind. People in every age have wondered how the body works. And in every age, they've tried to find answers.

For most of history, people had only one tool with which to study the body. That tool was the body itself. Their senses were their instruments. They listened to the heart and felt the heat of fever. They smelt the odour of decaying flesh or watched a wound heal. They studied healthy bodies and sick ones. In the 16th century, they began studying dead ones, too. Scientists peeled away flesh and fat to reveal muscle. They separated muscle from bone. They removed bones to examine the heart, lungs, liver and gut. Knowledge grew.

As tools improved, knowledge grew even further. Microscopes revealed cells. Machines gave doctors X-ray vision and recorded the rhythms of the heart. If you become a scientist, your tools will be even better, but you still won't have all the answers. The more people learn about the human body, the more there is to know. Amazing us.

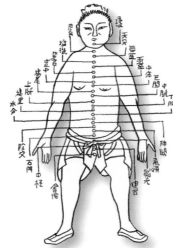

MYSTERIOUS FORCES
Chinese healers believe that life energy flows through invisible channels. They stimulate points in these channels in the body to treat illness and block pain. This practice is called acupuncture. No one knows why it works, but it often does.

HANDS ON

A New Look

How well do you know your body?.
Find a front-on photo of yourself. Hold a mirror at right angles to the picture. Tilt the mirror until you see the whole face. Now try the other side. Surprised? The two sides of your face are different. The closer you look at your body, the more you learn. The same is true for scientists. The closer they look at the human body, the more they discover about us.

BODY KNOWLEDGE
The ancients had little understanding of how the body worked. They blamed demons for illness. Today, we know that germs can cause illness. We know that our genes and habits influence health and growth.

AMAZING DISCOVERIES
In 1674, Anton van Leeuwenhoek discovered bacteria by cleaning his teeth. He put the stuff under a microscope he'd made and saw a world swarming with life. Two hundred years later, scientists realized that germs such as these could cause disease.

Word Builders

• **Anatomy** is the study of body parts. It comes from the Greek word, *anatome*, which means dissection.
• **Physiology** is the study of how body parts work. It comes from the Greek word *physis*, which means nature.

That's Amazing!

• Touch your thumb to your middle finger. No other animal can do that. This is one of the main things that distinguishes the human body.
• The oldest known human skeleton is Lucy. She was found in 1974 and is about 3.2 million years old.

Pathfinder

• In the Middle Ages, people believed that bad smells caused disease. What do we know about bad smells now? To find out, go to pages 24–25.
• Take a microscopic look inside the body to find out all about cells. Go to pages 10–11.
• Who discovered X-rays? How did this discovery change our understanding of bones? Find out on pages 40–41.

PAIN SAVER

Early surgeons could do little to relieve their patients' pain. In the 1840s, doctors discovered gases that allowed their patients to sleep right through surgery. We now know that anaesthetics like these block pain messages to the brain. Modern anaesthetics make long operations, like heart transplants, possible.

Cell City

YOU HAVE 75 BIILLION living factories inside you. These factories are your cells, some of the smallest units of life. They make up bone, skin, hair and every other part of you. If you could watch your cells work through a microscope, you'd see that they are constantly busy. They absorb nutrients from the fluid around them. They turn these nutrients into energy. They respond to messages from other cells. They churn out chemicals your body uses when you throw a ball, eat a burger or dream. Each cell completes billions of actions a second.

Like all living things, cells come into being, grow, reproduce and die. Unlike you, they don't need two parents. Cells are clones. They form when a single parent cell divides in two. This process is called mitosis. How often a cell divides and how long it lives depends upon its type. You have about 200 types of cell. Some, like skin cells, wear out quickly. They must be replaced quickly, too. They divide every 10 to 30 hours. Millions die and form every minute. Most brain cells, however, must last a lifetime. They do not reproduce. When you remember these words years from now, you'll use the same cells you're using today.

TEAM WORK

Cells are team players. They join with others like themselves to form tissues, and tissues form organs that together carry out life's work. Each cell's shape is perfect for its job. Most cells have a nucleus and the other parts shown in the drawing of the cell on page 11.

Nerve cells have long, tail-like structures called axons to carry messages from one nerve cell to the next.

Red blood cells look like Frisbees. They zip through your bloodstream, bringing oxygen to other cells and removing carbon dioxide.

Muscle cells are long and thin. They relax and contract as you move.

Fat cells look like bubble wrap. They protect your joints and some organs, store energy and provide warmth.

Skin cells fit together like bricks. They form a protective wall around your body.

INSIDE STORY

Wanted: DNA

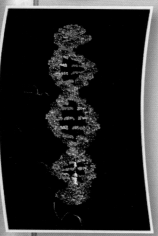

The Crime: David's bubblegum has been stolen.
The Evidence: A chewed piece of bubblegum stuck under Sally's desk.
Your Job: Find the thief. Impossible? Not with DNA testing. DNA (see left) is the chemical that makes up your genes. It is stored on 46 chromosomes that are twisted in pairs inside a cell's nucleus. Each nucleus holds a complete set of DNA. But the cell 'reads' only those genes it needs to do its job. Scientists can read a person's genes, too. All they need is a drop of saliva or a single hair, and a DNA sequencer. To solve your crime, match DNA from saliva on the gum with DNA from a suspect. You'll catch your thief!

Word Builders

Gene comes from *geneá*, the Greek word for 'generation' or race. Genes determine how you look. You inherit them from your parents. They are stored on 46 chromosomes, half from mum and half from dad. If you were a frog, you'd have 26 chromosomes. If you were a garden pea, you'd have 14. But simpler plants and animals don't always have fewer chromosomes. A goldfish has 94.

That's Amazing!

• All the DNA in your body could stretch to the Moon and back 37,585 times. It fits inside you because chromosomes have an amazing shape. They are like tightly coiled and twisted ladders. Unwind a metal spring to see how much space coils save.
• Blood cells live about 120 days. Liver cells live 18 months. Nerve cells can live for more than 100 years.

Pathfinder

• Sex cells (sperm and eggs) have only half the chromosomes of other cells. They form through a process called meiosis. Find out more about sex cells on pages 12–13.
• Red blood cells are the smallest cells in the body. Mature ones don't have a nucleus. Learn more about blood on pages 56–57.

Cell membrane. This gatekeeper lets supplies in, wastes and products out.

The parts of a cell are called **organelles**. Each has a different job.

Vacuoles. These storage vessels ferry supplies of nutrients.

Lysomes. The cell's digestive organs destroy wastes and dangerous substances.

Cytoplasm. This jelly-like maze of fibres throughout the cell supports organelles inside the cell.

Endoplasmic reticulum. The cell's proteins and fats move through these long tunnels.

Microtubules. These tracks transport chemicals and give the cell shape.

Ribosomes. These factories make proteins for the cell's use.

Nucleolus. This organelle makes and stores ribosomes.

Nucleus. The cell's 'brain' holds genes and directs cell activities.

Mitochondria. These powerhouses make energy to fuel cell activities.

Golgi bodies. These long sacs prepare cell products for export.

ALIENS ABOARD

Millions of beings call your body home. They live on your skin and inside you. They enter your body through food, air and cuts in your skin.

BAD BREATH?

B.O.? Blame bacteria. These one-cell beings can cause such problems and much worse. A few bacteria, like those pictured above, can become millions in hours. They destroy healthy tissue and keep the body from working properly.

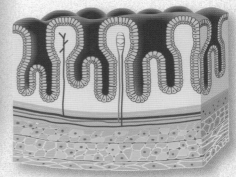

GOOD GUYS

Not all bacteria are bad. Good-guy bacteria in the folded lining of your stomach (pictured above) help your body use vitamins from foods. Some also fight their bad-guy cousins.

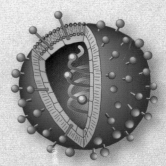

TRICKSTERS

Viruses invade your cells. They trick the cells into making more viruses. This process changes the cells chemically. They are damaged or die.

NASTY NEIGHBOURHOOD

Unlike healthy cells, there's no limit to the amount cancer cells divide. They invade normal cells, destroying healthy tissue.

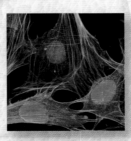

Elephant – 18 to 22 months
from conception till birth

Whale – 11 to 16 months
from conception till birth

Small bat – 40 to 60 days
from conception till birth

Life Begins

WHAT A MIRACLE you are! You began life as a single cell smaller than the dot on this *i*. But in less than a school year, you were born.

The story of you began with a sperm and an egg. Sperm and eggs are sex cells, or gametes. They form through a process called meiosis. Each carries 23 chromosomes, half the instructions for a human being. As a result of sexual intercourse, egg and sperm unite to form a new life. This is called conception.

Females are born with all the eggs they'll ever have. However, these eggs don't mature until puberty, which is the age of sexual maturity. Then, once a month, an egg bursts from the ovary in which it ripens. It slides into a Fallopian tube. It stays there for 10 to 15 hours, awaiting a sperm.

Males begin making sperm at puberty. Their testes, epididymus and seminal vesicles form an assembly line in which sperm develop, mature and are stored. During sex, males ejaculate. Semen, which is a mixture of fluid and sperm, shoots down the urethra and out of the penis, into the woman's vagina. The sperm then swim to the Fallopian tubes. Some 300 million sperm start this journey. Just a few hundred survive. Only one fertilizes the egg. From this tiny beginning, a baby forms and is born. The human race goes on.

PRIVATE PARTS

Some reproductive organs make the sperm or the eggs. Other organs transport them. Only one can house and nourish new life. This is the woman's uterus, or womb. Each month this 7.6 centimetre (3 in) wide organ gets ready to house new life. Its lining thickens. If no pregnancy occurs, the woman menstruates. She sheds this blood-rich lining. If pregnancy does occur, the lining combines with the placenta, which supplies nutrients to the unborn child. As the baby grows, the womb's muscles stretch. The cervix is the opening of the womb.

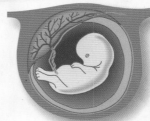

Seminal vesicles

Bladder

Vas deferens

Penis

Fluids from the seminal vesicles and **prostate** speed sperm along.

Epididymus

Testes

The vas deferens, **urethra** and penis form a sperm delivery system.

The sac-like **scrotum** holds the testes, which make sperm.

HANDS ON

Sweet Genes

How you look is determined by your genes. Like these sweets, genes for eye colour come in pairs. You inherit one gene from each parent. The front row of sweets represents this boy's parents. One parent has two brown-eye genes. The other has one brown-eye gene and one blue-eye gene. But both parents have brown eyes. Why? Here's a simple explanation: genes for darker eye colours are dominant over those for lighter colours. Get one of each, and you get the darker coloured eyes. The second row of sweets represents the boy and his siblings. What are their eye colours?

Use some coloured sweets or beads to give an imaginary family their genes for eye colour. If each parent has a brown-eye gene and a blue-eye gene, will any of the children have blue eyes?

FERTILIZATION
Sperm cells meet the egg and burrow in. The first sperm to penetrate fertilizes the egg. By hardening its outer wall, the egg locks out other sperm. The egg is now called a zygote.

IMPLANTATION
The zygote divides and divides again, but it does not grow in size. In about seven days, this tiny cell ball attaches to the wall of the uterus.

EMBRYO
At seven weeks, the unborn child is called an embryo. It grows quickly. Its umbilical cord brings the embryo oxygen and nutrients from the placenta.

Word Builders

Fraternal comes from the Latin word *frāternus*, which means 'brotherly'. **Fraternal twins** share the same womb but not the same genes. They develop when two sperm fertilize two eggs at the same time. **Identical twins** share the same genes. They develop when one fertilized egg splits in two and each half grows into a whole human being.

That's Amazing!

• Imagine swimming 40 kilometres (25 mi) in choppy seas. That's equivalent to the journey each sperm makes.
• Smell might guide sperm towards the egg. Sperm have odour receptors like those in the nose.
• Sperm develop best below body temperature. That's why the testes hang outside the body.

Pathfinder

• Your brain and spinal cord formed before almost all the rest of you. Learn more about these bundles of nerves on pages 14–15.
• The testes and ovaries make hormones that partly control sexual maturity. The story of your hormones is on pages 28–29.
• The muscled wall of the uterus stretches as the baby grows. Read more about muscles on pages 38–39.

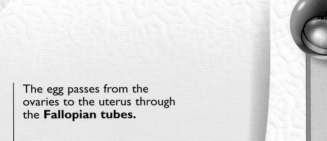

The egg passes from the ovaries to the uterus through the **Fallopian tubes.**

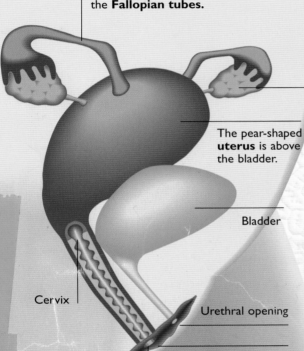

Ovary

The pear-shaped **uterus** is above the bladder.

Bladder

Cervix

Urethral opening

The lips of the **vulva** protect the vagina.

Vagina

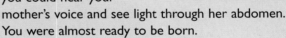

INSIDE STORY

Life on the Inside

That could be you on the screen. Like the baby-to-be on the ultrasound, you started life floating in your mother's womb. Warm amniotic fluid surrounded and protected you. Your umbilical cord delivered oxygen and food from your mother's blood. It also carried wastes away. Two months after conception, you were already on the move. You waved. You kicked. You sucked your thumb. By seven months, you could hear your mother's voice and see light through her abdomen. You were almost ready to be born.

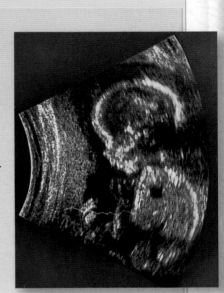

RECIPES FOR LIFE
Humans are more alike than not, but our genes make each of us unique. Sometimes, errors in genes or chromosomes cause major differences in the way humans look, think and act. This child has Down's syndrome caused by an extra chromosome.

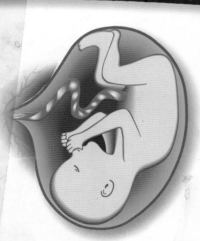

FOETUS
At two months, the embryo becomes a foetus. It has all its organs but isn't much bigger than a walnut. By seven months, it looks just like a baby and would be able to survive outside the womb.

HAPPY BIRTHDAY
At nine months, strong uterine movements push the baby through the vagina and into the world. The baby's first cry clears its lungs. It breathes.

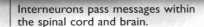

Interneurons pass messages within the spinal cord and brain.

Nerve Central

SHOULD YOU BREATHE? Should you digest your food? Should you sweat? You have no choice. These things happen automatically because of your nervous system. Should you dance, smile or shout? Now you're in control, thanks also to your nervous system. The nervous system is your body's decision and communication centre. It makes sure you respond appropriately to changes in your world.

Your nerves, brain and spinal cord make up your nervous system. Nerves reach from your brain to your face, eyes, ears, nose and spinal cord. They stretch from the spinal cord to every part of your body. All day, every day, sensory nerves gather information. They sense the warmth of the Sun. They detect changes in your body temperature or energy level. They send this information to your spinal cord, which speeds it to your brain. Your brain makes sense of the messages. It fires off a response. Motor nerves deliver the instructions. Your body acts.

Your brain and spinal cord are your central nervous system. Your nerves are the peripheral nervous system. Together, they control all the things you do without thinking and all those you do think about. Breathe, burp, blink or think – your busy nervous system is always hard at work.

Spinal cord

INSIDE STORY
Sensing the World

A breeze brushes your cheek. You hear a friend call. You inhale the woody scent of a campfire and lick sweet, sticky marshmallow from your lips. Special nerve cells bring you all the sensations of your world. They are sense cells called receptors. They change pressure, light, sound, scent or taste into electric pulses. Some receptors, such as the taste cells shown above, have hair-like parts that do the sensing. When the hairs come into contact with taste molecules from food, they send a signal to nearby nerves.

WHAT A NERVE!
Each nerve is made of thousands of nerve cells called neurons. These long, thin cells fire messages at amazing speeds – a nerve message can travel 91 metres (300 ft) a second. Electric pulses send each message down an axon, a neuron's long 'arm'. At the end of the axon, chemicals ferry the message across the tiny gap between nerve cells. The gap is called a synapse. The chemicals are neurotransmitters. The dendrites of the next cell receive the message. It is passed along in this way until it has reached its destination.

NIGHT DUTY
Your nervous system is on duty even as you sleep. It lets you breathe, turn and dream. It responds to danger signals and can wake you up.

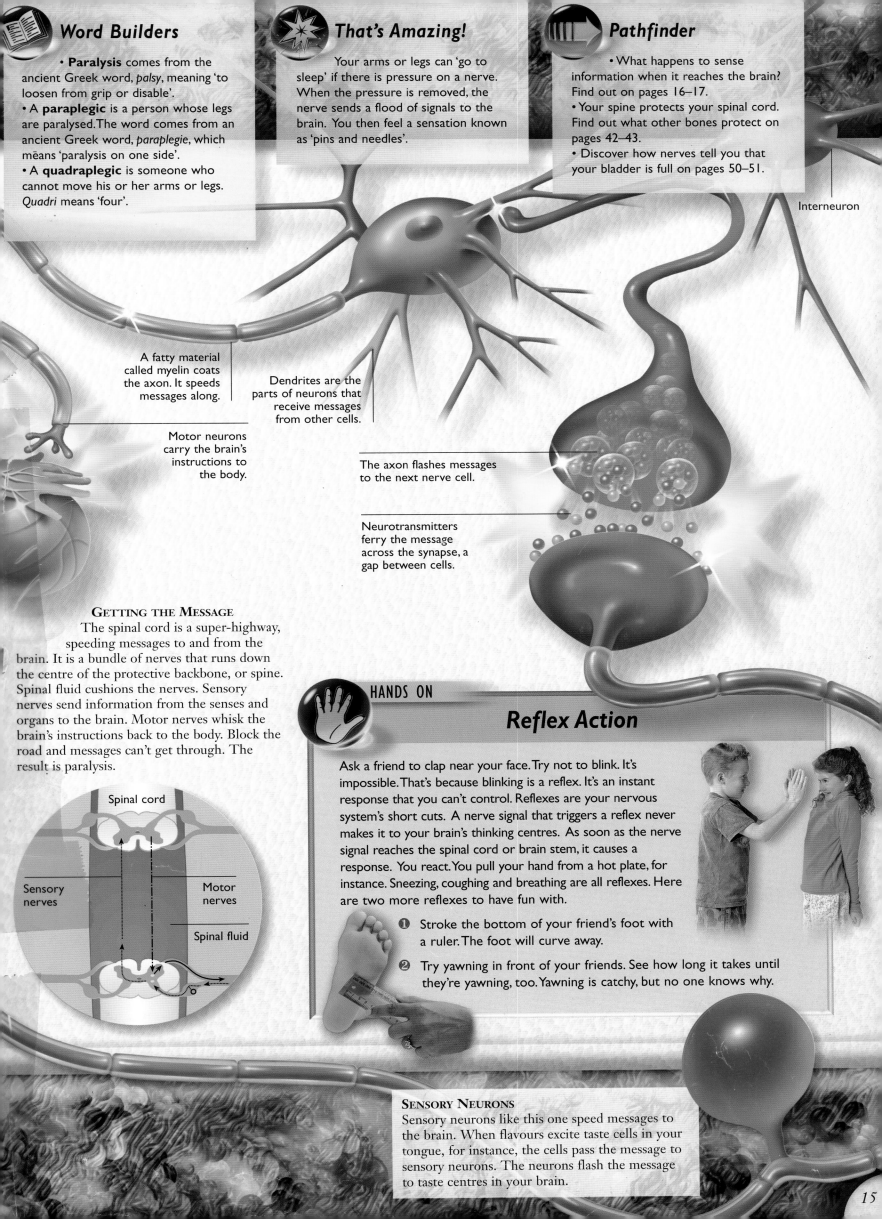

Word Builders

- **Paralysis** comes from the ancient Greek word, *palsy*, meaning 'to loosen from grip or disable'.
- A **paraplegic** is a person whose legs are paralysed. The word comes from an ancient Greek word, *paraplegie*, which mēans 'paralysis on one side'.
- A **quadraplegic** is someone who cannot move his or her arms or legs. *Quadri* means 'four'.

That's Amazing!

Your arms or legs can 'go to sleep' if there is pressure on a nerve. When the pressure is removed, the nerve sends a flood of signals to the brain. You then feel a sensation known as 'pins and needles'.

Pathfinder

- What happens to sense information when it reaches the brain? Find out on pages 16–17.
- Your spine protects your spinal cord. Find out what other bones protect on pages 42–43.
- Discover how nerves tell you that your bladder is full on pages 50–51.

Interneuron

A fatty material called myelin coats the axon. It speeds messages along.

Dendrites are the parts of neurons that receive messages from other cells.

Motor neurons carry the brain's instructions to the body.

The axon flashes messages to the next nerve cell.

Neurotransmitters ferry the message across the synapse, a gap between cells.

GETTING THE MESSAGE

The spinal cord is a super-highway, speeding messages to and from the brain. It is a bundle of nerves that runs down the centre of the protective backbone, or spine. Spinal fluid cushions the nerves. Sensory nerves send information from the senses and organs to the brain. Motor nerves whisk the brain's instructions back to the body. Block the road and messages can't get through. The result is paralysis.

Spinal cord

Sensory nerves

Motor nerves

Spinal fluid

HANDS ON

Reflex Action

Ask a friend to clap near your face. Try not to blink. It's impossible. That's because blinking is a reflex. It's an instant response that you can't control. Reflexes are your nervous system's short cuts. A nerve signal that triggers a reflex never makes it to your brain's thinking centres. As soon as the nerve signal reaches the spinal cord or brain stem, it causes a response. You react. You pull your hand from a hot plate, for instance. Sneezing, coughing and breathing are all reflexes. Here are two more reflexes to have fun with.

❶ Stroke the bottom of your friend's foot with a ruler. The foot will curve away.

❷ Try yawning in front of your friends. See how long it takes until they're yawning, too. Yawning is catchy, but no one knows why.

SENSORY NEURONS

Sensory neurons like this one speed messages to the brain. When flavours excite taste cells in your tongue, for instance, the cells pass the message to sensory neurons. The neurons flash the message to taste centres in your brain.

The Sensing Brain

TIP SEVERAL JIGSAW puzzles on the floor. Imagine that this is your world, a jumble of light and sound and ever-changing things around you. Now pick out just the pieces you need to make a picture. That's what your brain does hundreds of times a second. Your eyes, ears, nose, mouth and skin take in the world. But your brain makes sense of it. Your brain combines colours and smells, tastes and sounds, so you know the difference, for instance, between a skunk and a cat.

If you ever met a skunk, your senses awaken a great many nerve pathways to your brain. Information about the skunk's colour travels down one path. Messages about its size, shape or scent race down others. Each message lands in a separate area of the brain. These messages are like scattered puzzle pieces. But they don't stay separate long. Different brain regions have specialities, but they also work together. Your brain combines messages from all the senses and runs them through its memory banks. It tells you: 'Skunk!' Instructions zoom to your muscles: 'Don't move!' In less time than it takes to say 'Amazing!' your brain saves you from getting sprayed.

SMALL WONDER

Your brain weighs only 1.4 kilograms (3 lb). It looks like a wrinkled mass of grey jelly, but it's the world's most powerful information processor. It's made up of more than 100 thousand million nerve cells and 10 times as many support cells. It has three main parts: the cerebrum, cerebellum and brain stem. The cerebrum, which is the largest part of the brain, combines information from all your senses. It controls thought and action.

Sight

Hearing

The cerebellum controls balance and smooth movement.

Balance

The brain stem regulates vital life functions such as breathing.

The spinal cord connects your brain to the rest of your body.

HANDS ON

Picture This

Your memory and imagination rely on information from sound, touch, smell and taste as well as sight. How well do these senses serve you? Try this activity to find out.

Ask a friend to make a picture with clay. Don't look. Put on a blindfold, then trace the picture with your finger. Now take off your blindfold, but don't look. Draw what you felt. How do the pictures compare?

PAIN AND THE BRAIN

A cut scalp hurts. A cracked skull hurts. But injury to the brain doesn't. So what does the brain have to do with pain? Everything.

WARNING!

Special nerves carry pain messages to your brain. These nerves are in skin, muscle, blood vessels, bone and organs. They make sure you know when something's wrong.

SIGNAL SPEED

The sharp pain of a bee sting takes the fast lane to your brain. Signals sprint up 'fast' nerve fibres at up to 30 metres (100 ft) per second. Dull, aching pains move into awareness more slowly.

• There are more nerve cells in the human brain than stars in the Milky Way.
• Your brain's wrinkles may be ugly, but they're efficient. They pack more nerve cells into your skull.
• Information comes into the brain in pieces. It is also stored in pieces. Your brain stores colours separately from numbers, for instance.

• How do you remember that a skunk is a skunk and not a cat? Find out on pages 18–19.
• What connects your ear to your brain? Go to pages 22–23.
• Your brain uses 10 times as much energy as any other body part. Learn how energy-rich blood reaches the brain on pages 54–55.

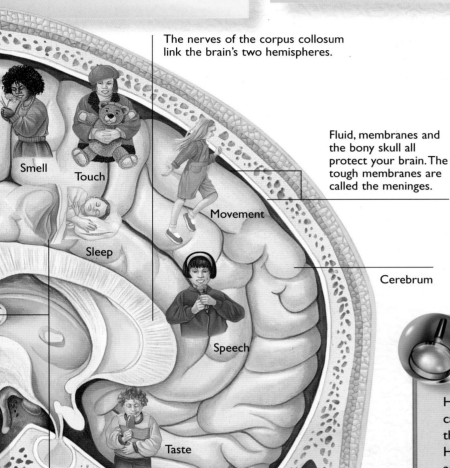

The nerves of the corpus collosum link the brain's two hemispheres.

Smell

Touch

Sleep

Movement

Fluid, membranes and the bony skull all protect your brain. The tough membranes are called the meninges.

Speech

Cerebrum

Taste

The pineal gland controls sleep.

Two for One

A deep furrow divides your cerebrum in two. The two halves, called hemispheres, have different specialities. The right one is good at spatial tasks, such as reading maps. In most people, the left is the seat of language. Each hemisphere controls the arm and leg on the opposite side of the body!

🔍 INSIDE STORY

Windows on the Brain

Frightened

Have you ever wondered why most adults can control reactions to emotions better than children? Scientists at McLean Hospital in the U.S.A. may have the answer. They showed teenagers and adults these pictures of frightened and worried faces. Then the scientists used brain imaging to record what happened in the brain as their subjects looked at the pictures. They found a difference. In teenagers, one of the brain's emotion centres responded more than the reasoning centre. In adults, the opposite was true. The younger the teenager, the greater the difference.

Worried

Natural Painkillers

Severe injury often causes no pain at first. That's because the brain makes its own painkillers. But these work only for a while. Pain is important. It forces you to rest the parts that hurt, which helps healing.

Nerve Blocks

Painkillers work in the brain. Some keep pain signals from getting through. They block the places on nerve cells that usually receive messages of pain. Others lessen reactions, such as swelling, that cause pain.

The Thinking Brain

YOUR BRAIN IS doing something amazing right now. It's reading about itself. Your dog's brain can't do that. Your cat's brain can't do it. And certainly your pet goldfish's can't.

The human brain is like no other. It can admire the stars and imagine life on other planets. It can design spaceships and send them to the Moon. It owes these remarkable abilities to the cerebrum. This walnut-like mass of nerve cells is more developed in humans than in any other animal. It is the largest part of your brain. It transforms the rush of information from your senses into thoughts, hopes and feelings. It makes you who you are.

Both genes and experience shape your brain. Genes determine the basic road map, the connections between nerve cells. But experience determines which 'roads' get used and which don't. When you practise your violin or read a bedtime story with your parent, some connections strengthen. As you learn new facts or skills, new connections form. You lose connections you do not use. This process continues throughout life. Scientists don't yet know what changes in the brain's cells to strengthen connections. Perhaps your cerebrum will someday work it out.

EMOTION AND LEARNING

Emotion is the glue that makes learning stick. You may love cricket but hate maths. If so, chances are you learn batting statistics more easily than times tables. Your pleasure helps you remember. Many parts of the brain play a role in this learning. The limbic system (parts of which are shown in yellow) and prefrontal area (in pink) are important ones. The limbic system is the group of brain areas in which emotions form. Emotions are combined with thoughts in the prefrontal area.

HANDS ON
Shaping Memory

Glance at the shapes to the left (A). Now glance at those below left (B). You'll probably remember the bottom ones longer. Here's why: You have two types of memory. Working memory lasts a minute or so. It lets you remember a message to give your brother, for instance. Long-term memory is your brain's hard disc. What it records can last a lifetime. To enter long-term memory, however, an experience needs to be repeated and linked to other, similar items. The house shape has more staying power because it's familiar.

A

B

ACCIDENTAL KNOWLEDGE
Ouch! A rod damaged poor Phineas Gage's frontal lobe, changing his personality. From this accident, scientists learnt that the frontal lobes help control emotion.

WHEN THE BRAIN BREAKS

Illness can damage the brain areas involved in thinking and feeling. These mental illnesses often change a person's behaviour and personality. Most cannot be cured, but many can be treated.

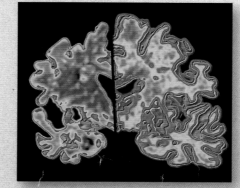

CHANGING PICTURES
People once thought mental illness was 'all in the head'. It isn't. It's as real as a broken ankle or chicken pox. The brain scan on the left is from a person with Alzheimer's disease. The one on the right is from a healthy person. The Alzheimer's brain is much smaller because the disease kills brain cells. Images like these are helping scientists to see how the brain changes during mental illness. New knowledge will lead to better treatments.

Cerebrum is the Latin word for 'brain'. **Cerebellum** is Latin for 'little brain'. The word cerebral comes from the Latin, too. It means 'of or relating to the brain'. **Cerebral** also means 'relating to the intellect'. When you puzzle over a difficult problem, you're being cerebral, or intellectual. You're putting your cerebrum to good use.

• Babies who are neglected have brains that are 20–30 per cent smaller than those who are well cared for.
• Words shape the brain. The more an infant hears each day, the more likely he or she will learn well later on.
• Children who learn two languages from birth store them in the same brain centre. When someone learns a second language later on in life, the brain stores it separately.

• One nerve fibre connects your brain to every two eye muscles. What else can you learn about how the eye works? Go to pages 20–21.
• Brain cells die as you get older. Can you keep learning without them? Find out on pages 30–31.
• Your brain helps you decide what to eat and when to eat. Then a different 'brain' in the digestive system takes over. If you want to know more, turn to pages 48–49.

Go to pages 20–21. ... Find out on pages 30–31. ... turn to pages 48–49.

INSIDE STORY

Famous Mind

Not all brain diseases damage the mind. Stephen Hawking has ALS, or Lou Gehrig's disease. This disease attacks nerve cells connecting the brain to the spinal cord. Like Hawking, people with ALS have trouble walking and speaking, but their minds are fine. Hawking, one of the greatest physicists ever, has done most of his work since becoming ill.

I KNEW IT!

People can't read minds, but we do get 'hunches', or gut feelings. Our brains seem to know something before we do. Scientists suspect this is because our brains remember experiences and emotions we only think we've forgotten.

COMMON ILLNESS
The most common mental illness is depression. It drains happiness, hope and laughter from life. Many people with this disease lead successful lives. Abraham Lincoln was one.

DIFFERENT BRAINS
Some victims of crime or war cannot forget these terrible events. The memories invade without warning. Other people have had similar experiences but don't have the same problem. Scans show that the brains of these two groups are different.

The Eyes Have It

YOUR EYES GLANCE up to watch a bird. They dart right and left as you cross a street. They adjust automatically to the dim light of dusk and the bright light of the summer sun. They focus on objects near and far. Protected within their bony nest, your eyes are always on the move, feeding your curious brain.

Light bounces off every object in your sight. Your eyes gather and focus this light. They then transform it into millions of nerve signals. These hurtle down the optic nerve to your brain at 400 kilometres (248 mi) per hour. When your brain interprets the messages, you see.

The world you see and the one your eyes record are not identical. The back of your eyeball, which is called the retina, is covered with light-sensing cells called rods and cones. Rods detect movement and let you see in dim light. Cones provide clear, sharp, colour vision. The cones cluster together in the macula, which is the centre of your retina. Only this part of your eye records detailed images. Your brain fills in the rest from memory. Though your eyes focus light, your brain makes sense of what your eyes record. Can't find your maths book even though you're staring right at it? Your brain, not your eyes, is at fault.

NATURE'S LAUNDRY
Each blink sweeps cleansing tears across your eyes. These tears contain germ-fighting chemicals. They form in the tear, or lacrimal, glands above your eye and wash out through tear ducts into your nose.

NO GYM NEEDED
Your eyes get a constant workout. Six muscles move each eyeball every time you move your gaze. Other muscles adjust the lens and pupil. These are always on the move to keep your world in focus.

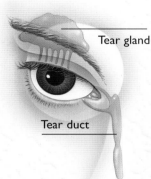

Tear gland

Tear duct

HOW WE SEE
Light bends as it passes through the cornea. It then enters the pupil and hits the lens. The lens thins to focus far-off objects and thickens for close-up ones. Then the lens projects an upside-down image on the retina, which changes the image into nerve signals. Your brain reads the signals and shows you the world the right way up.

INSIDE STORY
Windows on the Soul

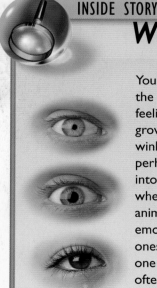

Your eyes are two-way windows. They show you the world, but they also show others your feelings. Raised upper lids signal surprise. Pupils grow wide with wonder, interest or fear. You might wink to let someone know you're kidding and perhaps blink when you're nervous. You may gaze into the eyes of those you love, but look away when embarrassed or ashamed. You can cry. All animals have tears, but only humans cry from emotion. Emotional tears are not like natural ones. They're made up of different chemicals. No one knows how emotional tears help, but people often feel better after a good cry.

NORMAL VISION
When the lens focuses light directly on the retina, a person can see clearly. Genes, illness and ageing can interfere with normal vision.

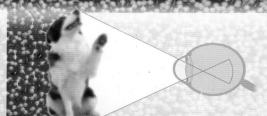

SHORT SIGHTED
The shape of some people's eyes makes light focus in front of their retina. Objects far away look blurry.

Word Builders

- The **iris**, which is the coloured part of the eye, gets its name from the ancient Greek rainbow goddess, Iris.
- The gel that gives the eye its shape is called **vitreous** because it is clear. **Vitreous** comes from the Latin word *vireus*, which means 'glassy'.
- A protective membrane lines the eyelid, then covers the eyeball. It is called the **conjunctiva**, from the Latin word *conjunctus*, which means 'joined'.

That's Amazing!

- The spot on the retina where nerves meet has no light-sensing cells. It's your blind spot.
- Your fingerprints have 40 features that are unique to you. Your iris has 266. It's the perfect ID. Will eye scans someday eye-dentify you?
- You can't see for one-half hour a day. Why? You're blinking.

Pathfinder

- You inherit eye colour from your parents. How does this work? Find out on pages 12–13.
- Eye colour comes from a pigment called melanin. So does skin colour. For more on melanin, turn to pages 34–35.
- Someone who is blind must rely on other senses. Hearing, especially, becomes very strong. Take a look at ears on pages 22–23.

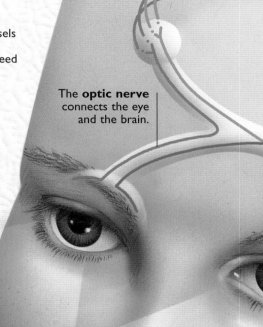

The gel-like **vitreous humour** gives the eye its shape.

The clear **cornea** helps focus light.

The **retina** converts the image into nerve signals.

Blood vessels in the **choroid** feed the retina.

The **optic nerve** connects the eye and the brain.

The **lens** focuses the image.

The **sclera** is the tough white coating of the eyeball.

Light enters through the dark opening of the **pupil**.

The **iris muscle** controls how much light gets in.

HANDS ON

Eye Can't Believe It!

Your eyes are in different positions, so they record slightly different images. Your brain combines these to create a single image with depth. See how this works. Hold a tube to your right eye. Place your left hand as shown. Look straight ahead. One eye sees your hand. The other sees the hole. What does your brain see? A hole in your hand.

Rod

Cone

SEEING COLOUR

The three types of cone cell in your retina detect red, blue and green. Light stimulates different combinations of these cones to produce all the colours you see. In some people, one type of cone cell is missing or faulty. The person can't see that colour. We say that he or she is colour-blind.

LONG SIGHTED

As people age, the eye's lens stiffens, and it cannot focus on close objects. Light falls behind the retina, causing close objects to look blurry.

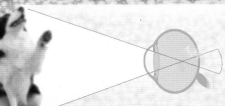

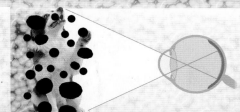

DIABETIC BLINDNESS

Diabetes can damage blood vessels in the retina. The damaged parts can't send messages to the brain. This can be treated.

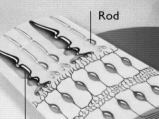

How We Hear

HOLD THE PALM of your hand close to your mouth and then talk. Do you feel the vibrations? These vibrations are the sound waves of your voice. All sound travels in invisible waves. Your ear collects and moves these sound waves from the air to your brain. Here's how.

Sound waves rush into the collecting bowl of your outer ear and then travel down the ear canal. There, they bump into the eardrum, making it vibrate. These vibrations carry the sound into your middle ear. The middle ear is a small, air-filled space that contains three tiny bones smaller than a 1p coin. These bones connect to the eardrum and to one another. When the eardrum moves, so do the bones. Their movement strengthens the sound waves, allowing you to hear even very quiet sounds. The movement also sends the sound into a part of the inner ear called the cochlea. Here, special cells change sound waves into nerve signals. The signals pass down the hearing nerve to your brain. When your brain interprets the nerve signals, you hear.

The inner ear also houses your body's balance system. The balance system tells your brain when your head moves. If it didn't, you'd get dizzy reading this page. How about that? You use your ears to read.

THE EAR–BRAIN CONNECTION
Millions of hair cells line the cochlea. These are the sense cells that turn sound waves into nerve signals. When sound waves wash into the cochlea, they ripple through a fluid. These ripples make the hair cells sway, releasing their signals. The signals pulse down tiny nerve fibres at the bottom of each cell. These fibres combine to form the auditory (or hearing) nerve, which travels to the brain.

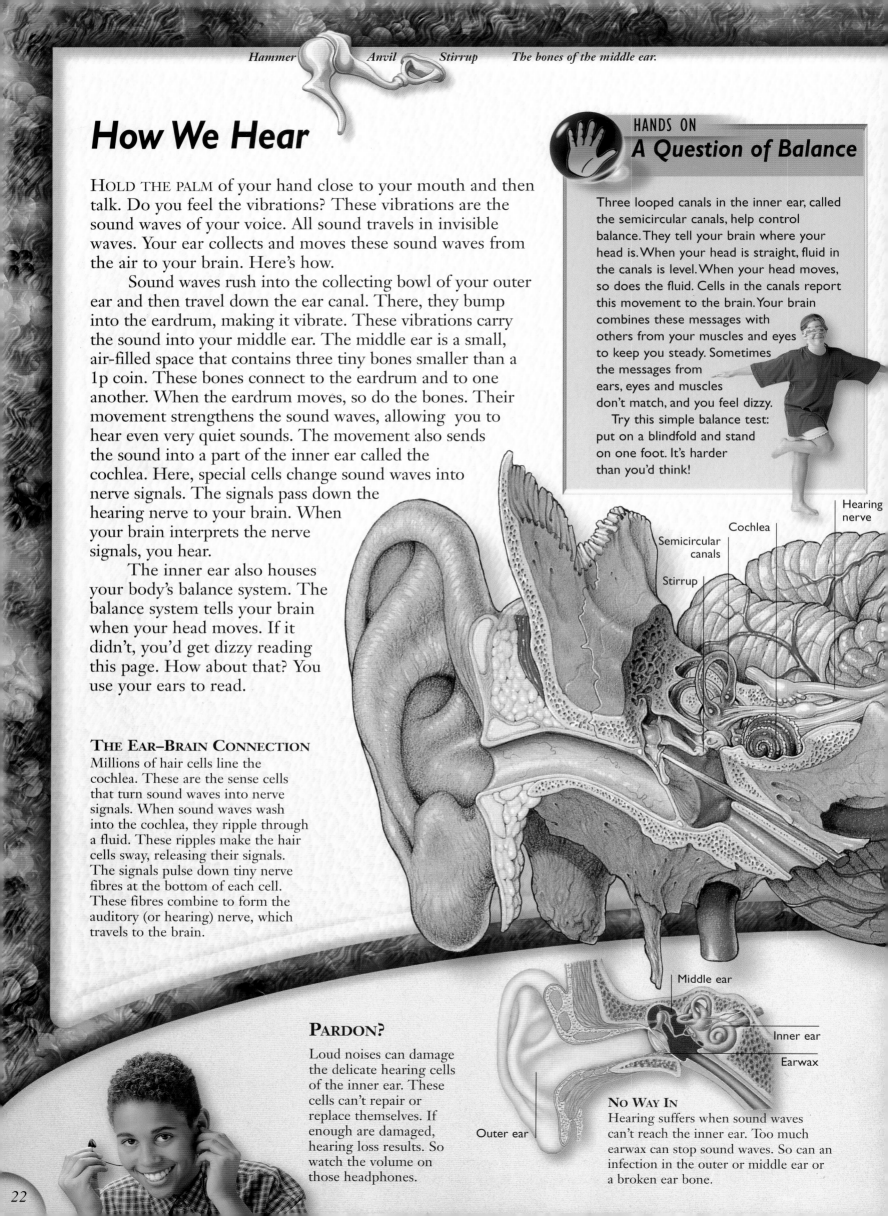

HANDS ON
A Question of Balance

Three looped canals in the inner ear, called the semicircular canals, help control balance. They tell your brain where your head is. When your head is straight, fluid in the canals is level. When your head moves, so does the fluid. Cells in the canals report this movement to the brain. Your brain combines these messages with others from your muscles and eyes to keep you steady. Sometimes the messages from ears, eyes and muscles don't match, and you feel dizzy.

Try this simple balance test: put on a blindfold and stand on one foot. It's harder than you'd think!

Hearing nerve

Cochlea

Semicircular canals

Stirrup

Middle ear

Inner ear

Earwax

PARDON?
Loud noises can damage the delicate hearing cells of the inner ear. These cells can't repair or replace themselves. If enough are damaged, hearing loss results. So watch the volume on those headphones.

Outer ear

NO WAY IN
Hearing suffers when sound waves can't reach the inner ear. Too much earwax can stop sound waves. So can an infection in the outer or middle ear or a broken ear bone.

📖 Word Builders

• The word **cochlea** means 'snail' in Latin. Take a look at the shape of the cochlea to see how the part got its name.
• The **eustachian tube** was named after the Italian anatomist Bartolomeo Eustachio. He published studies of the ear in the 1560s. He described the tube better than anyone before him.

✦ That's Amazing!

• Sound waves in the air travel 1.6 kilometres (1 mi) in five seconds.
• Tiny glands in your ear canals make wax. The sticky wax traps dust and germs, protecting your ear.
• Your voice sounds different on a tape recorder because the sound reaches you only through the air. When you talk, some of the sound travels through the bones of your skull.

📖 Pathfinder

• The ear's eustachian tube leads to the throat. Where does the throat lead? Find out on pages 26–27.
• The bones in the ear are the smallest in the body. Where are the longest bones in your body? Go to pages 40–41.
• A mucous membrane lines your middle ear. What does mucus do for you? Turn to pages 24–25.

HEAR, FIDO

Dogs and many other mammals have wide, flattened ear flaps to help them pick up a variety of sounds. They can 'prick' their outer ears, moving them to catch sound waves. Our outer ears cannot move. They are shaped to capture passing sound waves. Shape isn't the only difference between dog and human ears. A dog's hearing is sharper. We can't hear many of the high, squeaky sounds or low, rumbling ones that Fido can.

RESTORING HEARING

People who can't hear very much, or can't hear at all, can be helped by a device called a cochlear implant. A microphone and speech processor are worn behind the ear. They pick up sounds and turn them into electrical signals. These signals pass through the skin to a part of the device that is implanted inside the inner ear. The implant sends the signals on to the brain.

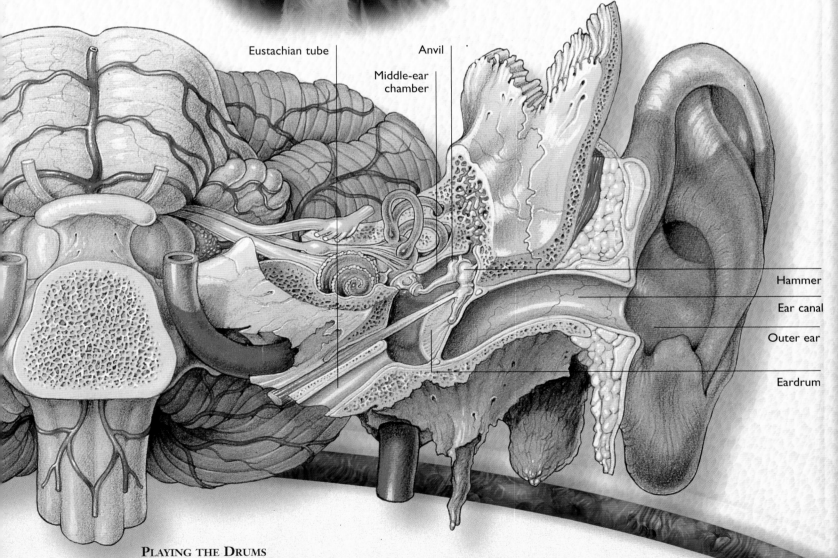

Eustachian tube — Anvil

Middle-ear chamber

Hammer

Ear canal

Outer ear

Eardrum

PLAYING THE DRUMS

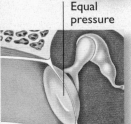

Equal pressure

Air inside the ear canal pushes against the eardrum. At the same time, air inside the middle ear pushes back. When the pressure on both sides is the same, the eardrum works normally. It vibrates, passing sound from the outer to the middle ear.

BAD VIBRATIONS

Eardrum balloons

The eustachian tube lets air from the nose into the middle ear. If the tube can't open, the pressure of air in the middle ear is no longer the same as in the ear canal. The eardrum suddenly balloons. Ouch! It can't work well and you can't hear properly.

RELIEF!

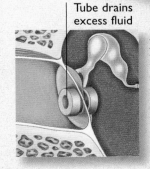

Tube drains excess fluid

During a middle-ear infection, fluid presses against the eardrum. It hurts. Doctors can insert tiny tubes to drain the fluid.

The Nose Knows

WANT TO KNOW about mucus and nose hairs? Before you say 'Yuck!' and turn the page, consider this. Without mucus, you couldn't enjoy the scent of a rose. Without nose hairs, objects like dust, pollen and tiny flying things would get right up your nose.

Your nose has two important jobs. It cleans and warms the air you breathe. It also brings you life's odours – foul and sweet. Your nose is well made for these tasks. It sticks out from your face to take in air. It has blood vessels inside to warm the air passing through. It is protected high up by bone, but it has flexible cartilage at the tip. The cartilage lets you widen your nostrils to breathe more deeply.

Your nose filters enough air each day to fill 500 balloons. Nose hairs allow air in but keep debris out. Bits of pollen or dirt small enough to sneak by can trigger a sneeze. Otherwise they suffer the same fate as germs, which mucus inside your nose traps and helps destroy. Mucus also dissolves scent molecules so that you can smell. It saves you from drinking sour milk or wearing yesterday's socks. So now you know about mucus and nose hairs. It wasn't as bad as you thought, was it?

INSIDE STORY
Ah-ah-ah-choooo!

Dust mites are just one of the unwelcome visitors that can make you sneeze. They're microscopic animals that live in dust (this one's enlarged so you can see it). If mites irritate your mucous membrane, nerve cells there sound an alarm. Your brain's breathing centre responds. It signals to the lungs. They fill with air. *Ah-ah-ah....* Then the air passages close. Pressure builds up until – *chooo!* Air explodes from your lungs with hurricane force, taking mites and mucus with it.

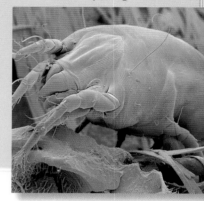

HANDS ON
Yum! Smells Good

If you love chocolate, thank your nose! Much of what you experience as taste is really smell. The same molecules in food trigger both senses. Your nose is at least 20,000 times more sensitive than your tongue. Find out for yourself.

❶ Hold your nose while you eat a piece of chocolate. You'll taste the sweetness but not the flavour. Now do the same while chewing an apple and then a carrot. Can you tell the difference between the two?

❷ To make a taste stronger, breathe out through your nose after swallowing. When you breathe out, scent molecules travel from your mouth to the smell area in your nose.

HOW WE SMELL
Flowers, dogs, cabbage, people – all of these things give off different scent molecules. The scent molecules travel through the air into your nose. At the top of your nose, under the bridge, they bump into smell cells. Odours from cabbage will turn on one set of smell cells. Odours from dogs or people will turn on others. The turned-on cells send messages to one of your olfactory bulbs. These are two button-sized clumps of nerve cells just above the smell receptors. They relay messages between your nose and brain. Your brain combines thousands of scent messages into a single smell, then compares this odour with those already on file. Mmm! Smell that rose.

SMELLY BUSINESS
Few smells please, or displease, all people all of the time. A person's genes and upbringing influence what smells good or bad. So does experience. A sewage worker might not even notice smells that others think are foul.

SMELLS WELCOME
Your smell cells occupy two patches about the size of raisins, high in your nose. They stretch hair-like cilia through the mucous membrane to detect smells. Smell cells can pick up about 1,000 different odours.

• The **olfactory** bulbs, which contain your smell cells, get their name from the Latin word *olfactorius*, which means 'to get a smell of'.
• The word **nasal** describes anything to do with the nose. It even refers to the part of a helmet that protects the nose, which is called a nasal. Nasal comes from the Latin word for 'nose', which is *nasalis*.

• You have a sixth sense – the common chemical sense. Nerve endings in your eyes, nose and mouth detect the heat of spicy foods and the sting of onions.
• Doctors can use odours to help diagnose diseases. Typhoid smells like bread, and gangrene like rotten apples.
• A mother can recognize her baby by smell alone. A baby uses odours, too. That's how he finds his mother's nipple.

• Smell messages pass through the brain's memory centre. Read more about memory on pages 18–19.
• Your nose makes about 1 litre (1 qt) of mucus a day. Tiny, hair-like cilia sweep old mucus towards your throat. What happens then? Find out on pages 26–27.
• The air you breathe lands in your lungs. Go to pages 52–53 to learn more.

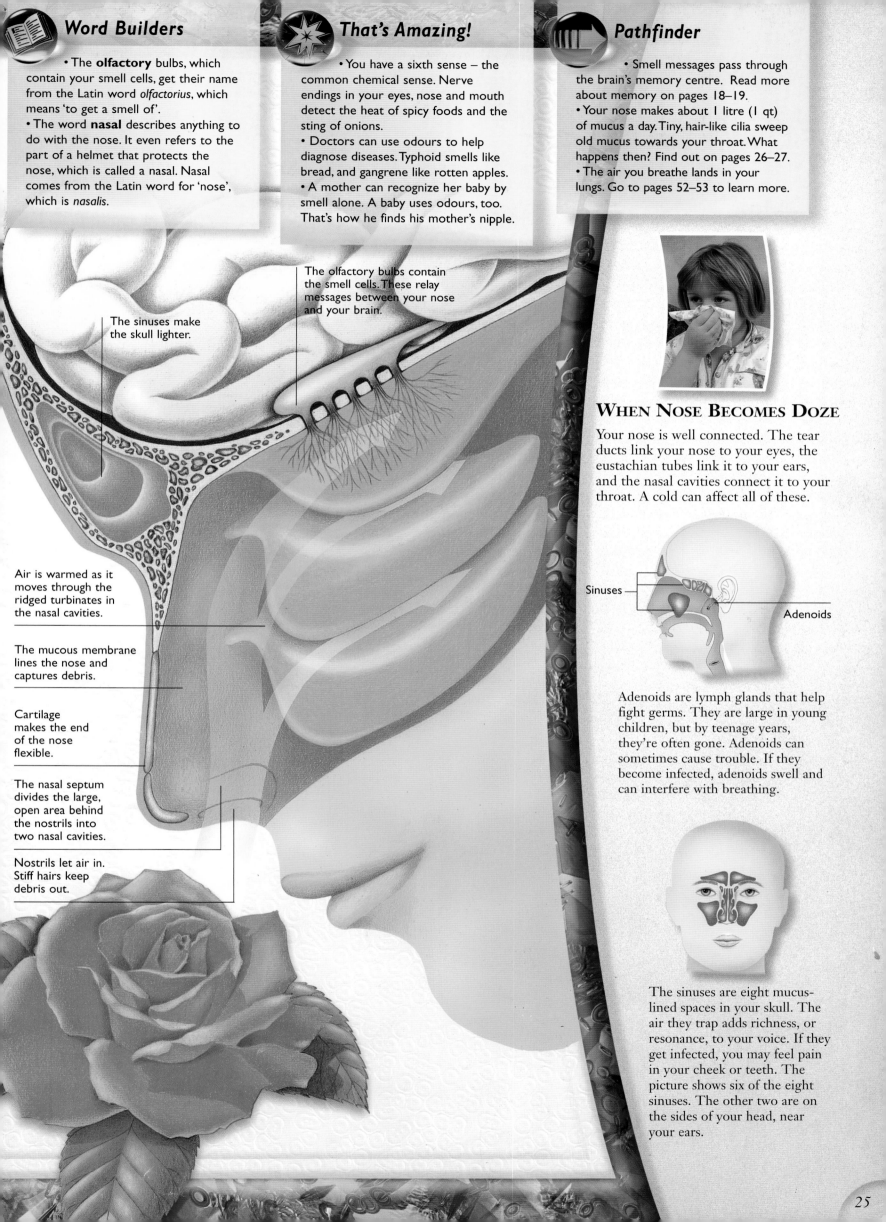

The sinuses make the skull lighter.

The olfactory bulbs contain the smell cells. These relay messages between your nose and your brain.

Air is warmed as it moves through the ridged turbinates in the nasal cavities.

The mucous membrane lines the nose and captures debris.

Cartilage makes the end of the nose flexible.

The nasal septum divides the large, open area behind the nostrils into two nasal cavities.

Nostrils let air in. Stiff hairs keep debris out.

WHEN NOSE BECOMES DOZE

Your nose is well connected. The tear ducts link your nose to your eyes, the eustachian tubes link it to your ears, and the nasal cavities connect it to your throat. A cold can affect all of these.

Sinuses

Adenoids

Adenoids are lymph glands that help fight germs. They are large in young children, but by teenage years, they're often gone. Adenoids can sometimes cause trouble. If they become infected, adenoids swell and can interfere with breathing.

The sinuses are eight mucus-lined spaces in your skull. The air they trap adds richness, or resonance, to your voice. If they get infected, you may feel pain in your cheek or teeth. The picture shows six of the eight sinuses. The other two are on the sides of your head, near your ears.

These are the organs of the throat.
If infected, tonsils and adenoids can be removed.

Tonsils   Adenoids   Uvula

Down the Hatch

YOUR TONGUE IS hairy. That's not an insult. It's a fact. Millions of microscopic 'gustatory hairs' cover your tongue. These aren't real hairs. They're tips of taste cells, which cluster in onion-shaped bunches called taste buds. Your taste buds are too small to see, but stick out your tongue and you'll see a landscape of bumps called papillae. These house your taste buds as well as the nerve endings that scream 'Hot!' when you attack a pizza.

While your tongue's out, look around your mouth. The tissue dangling from the back of your throat is your uvula. It closes the nasal passage when you swallow. The dark tube beyond the uvula is your pharynx, or throat. Food and air start their downwards journey there. Lift your tongue to see your frenulum. This membrane anchors the tongue.

Your teeth and palate are more familiar. Your teeth cut and mash food. They mix it with saliva to form a bolus, the lump you swallow. Your tongue, lips and cheek muscles push the bolus along your palate. From there, it slides into your throat. Together, your mouth and throat support some of your body's most vital and enjoyable functions. They let you breathe, eat, speak and savour a slice of pizza.

How We Speak

Your lips aren't all that move when you speak. Your vocal cords do, too. The vocal cords are two springy bands at the opening of your larynx, or voice box. They form a V-shape. Air from your lungs flows through this opening. When you breathe, the V is open. When you speak, it narrows. Air causes the vocal cords to vibrate, creating sound. The more forceful the air, the louder the sound.

Larynx

Vocal cords

Although vocal cords produce sound, the mouth creates speech. Your teeth, tongue and lips shape raw sounds into consonants and vowels. Air spaces in your skull give your voice its own unique tone.

You can feel your larynx at the very top of your throat. It is made up of nine cartilages. The biggest of these is the thoracic cartilage, or Adam's apple. Your vocal cords attach to the Adam's apple and to the smaller cartilages behind it.

Gulp!

Your body has a life-saving trapdoor. It's a flap of cartilage above your windpipe called the epiglottis. When you swallow, the epiglottis swings shut, closing the windpipe so no food gets in. Place your fingers on your throat. The ridges you feel are your air passage. Now swallow. The saliva goes down your food tube, or oesophagus, which lies behind the windpipe. The oesophagus is a muscled tube. When you swallow, the muscles tighten and relax, sending food or saliva downwards.

Epiglottis open

Epiglottis shut

PUCKER UP
Call them smoochers, smackers, or just plain lips – but you wouldn't want to be without them. You use your lips to eat, to seal your mouth closed while you chew and to shape sounds so you can speak. Just try talking with them closed. Your lips are also the body's most sensitive thermometer. They detect food that's too hot or cold. And do you want to whistle or kiss? Well, pucker up!

THE MIGHTY TONGUE
Your tongue is a mighty and mobile muscle. It licks, lifts and darts as it forms sounds, moves food or teases your brother. It also springs up to guard your throat against objects that could choke you.

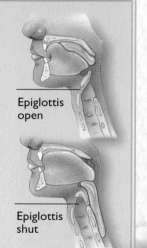

SAY 'AHHH'
A peep at your throat reveals lots about your health, but your doctor must first get your tongue out of the way. Then the doctor can spot infection in your throat or tonsils. With a special tool called a laryngoscope, he or she can check your voice box, too. Tonsil infections are most common in childhood.

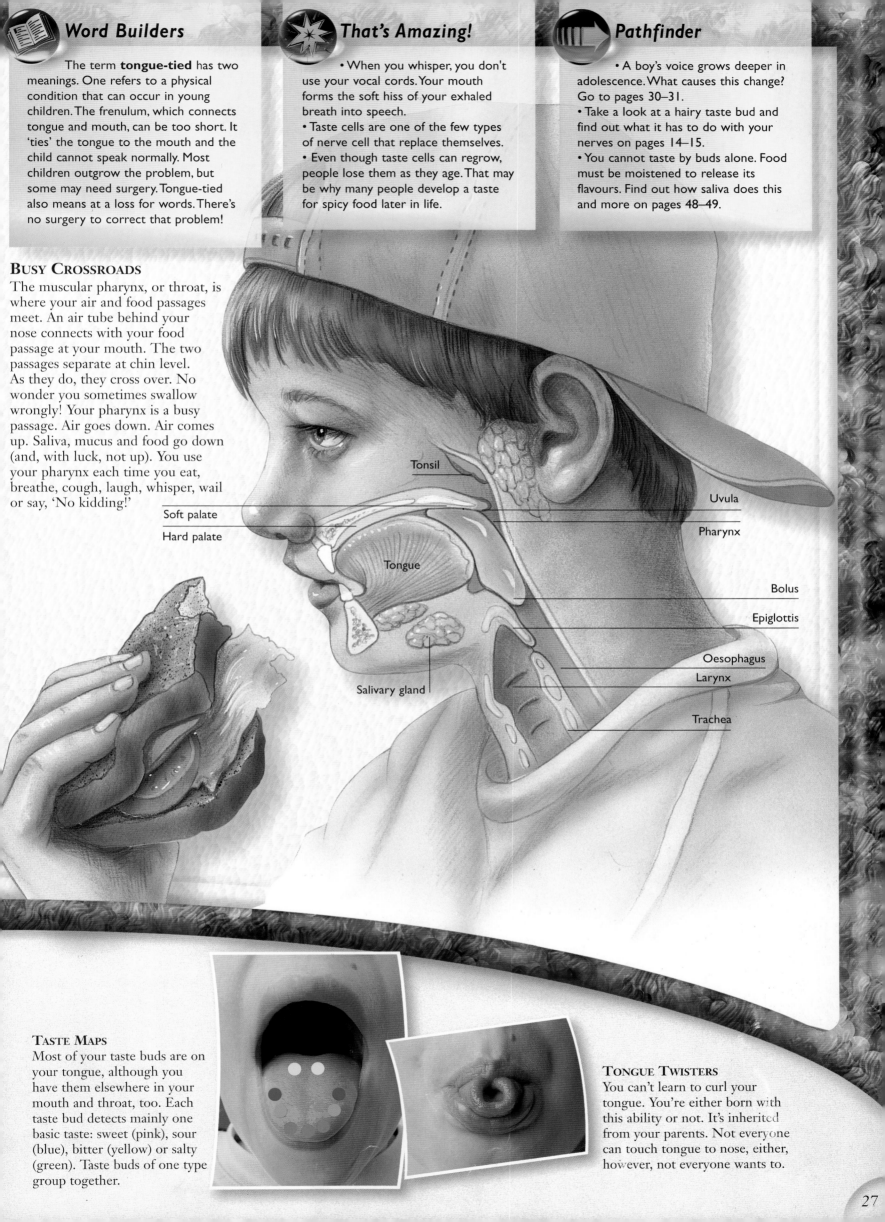

Word Builders

The term **tongue-tied** has two meanings. One refers to a physical condition that can occur in young children. The frenulum, which connects tongue and mouth, can be too short. It 'ties' the tongue to the mouth and the child cannot speak normally. Most children outgrow the problem, but some may need surgery. Tongue-tied also means at a loss for words. There's no surgery to correct that problem!

That's Amazing!

• When you whisper, you don't use your vocal cords. Your mouth forms the soft hiss of your exhaled breath into speech.
• Taste cells are one of the few types of nerve cell that replace themselves.
• Even though taste cells can regrow, people lose them as they age. That may be why many people develop a taste for spicy food later in life.

Pathfinder

• A boy's voice grows deeper in adolescence. What causes this change? Go to pages 30–31.
• Take a look at a hairy taste bud and find out what it has to do with your nerves on pages 14–15.
• You cannot taste by buds alone. Food must be moistened to release its flavours. Find out how saliva does this and more on pages 48–49.

BUSY CROSSROADS

The muscular pharynx, or throat, is where your air and food passages meet. An air tube behind your nose connects with your food passage at your mouth. The two passages separate at chin level. As they do, they cross over. No wonder you sometimes swallow wrongly! Your pharynx is a busy passage. Air goes down. Air comes up. Saliva, mucus and food go down (and, with luck, not up). You use your pharynx each time you eat, breathe, cough, laugh, whisper, wail or say, 'No kidding!'

Tonsil

Soft palate

Hard palate

Tongue

Uvula

Pharynx

Bolus

Epiglottis

Oesophagus

Larynx

Salivary gland

Trachea

TASTE MAPS

Most of your taste buds are on your tongue, although you have them elsewhere in your mouth and throat, too. Each taste bud detects mainly one basic taste: sweet (pink), sour (blue), bitter (yellow) or salty (green). Taste buds of one type group together.

TONGUE TWISTERS

You can't learn to curl your tongue. You're either born with this ability or not. It's inherited from your parents. Not everyone can touch tongue to nose, either, however, not everyone wants to.

Chemical Messengers

YOU CAN IMPRESS the next adult who says, 'My, how you've grown.' Just answer, 'Yes. It's my hormones.' Hormones are chemical messengers. Along with your nervous system, they keep your body in balance. They aid digestion and adjust body temperature. They help keep blood pressure steady. Hormones also regulate growth and reproduction. A boy's voice deepens. A girl's breasts grow. A woman's ovary releases an egg. You grow taller. Hormones are at work.

Some hormones form in organs called endocrine glands. Others form in body tissues, such as the stomach or heart. Most of these hormones travel through your bloodstream to other body parts. Once they reach their targets, they cause changes. You feel the results when you get hungry, thirsty or tired, for instance. When you eat, drink or sleep, you bring your body back in balance.

A part of your brain called the hypothalamus monitors many hormones. If it detects too much of one, it alerts your pituitary gland. The pituitary sends a message to the gland that makes that hormone: Slow down! It does. If levels drop too low, the brain nudges the pituitary again and the cycle repeats. Your brain and hormones work together to keep your body running.

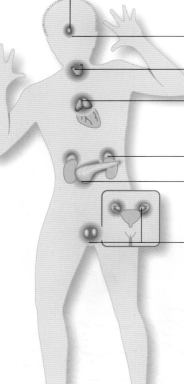

Chief controller, the **hypothalamus**.

The **pituitary** controls other glands and regulates growth.

The **thyroid** influences growth and energy.

The **thymus** makes a hormone that influences the body's defences.

The **adrenals** make adrenalin and regulate the balance of water and salt.

The **pancreas** makes insulin, a hormone that helps control blood sugar.

The **testes** in men and **ovaries** in women make sex hormones.

IN CONTROL

Seven main glands control many of the activities that keep your body running day in and day out.

INSIDE STORY

Life-Saving Hormones

This girl is saving her own life. She has a disease called Type 1 diabetes and is giving herself an injection of insulin. Without this daily treatment, she would die. Insulin is made in the pancreas. It helps the body turn blood sugar into energy.

People with Type 1 diabetes don't make any insulin. That's why they need daily injections. This disease starts in childhood. Another Type of diabetes, Type 2, usually develops late in life. People with Type 2 diabetes make insulin, but their bodies can't use it properly.

A FRIENDSHIP HORMONE?

Can a hormone make you want to be with other people? Maybe. Just as one hormone prepares the body to fight, so another helps it relax. This hormone is called oxytocin. It causes changes in a mother's body that help her to be calm and let her nurse her baby. All people, not just nursing mothers, have oxytocin in their body. Some scientists think the hormone is at work when you feel like being with other people.

DAILY MESSAGES

Are you feeling hungry or tired? Do you have a cut that is healing or an insect bite that's swelling? Hormones and other chemical messengers play a role in each of these experiences.

HUNGER

At least three hormones curb appetite. One of these, urocortin, may shut off hunger during times of stress.

CLOTTING

Blood platelets, a type of blood cell, make a chemical messenger that helps blood clot. It's called thromboxane. It causes the platelets to stick together.

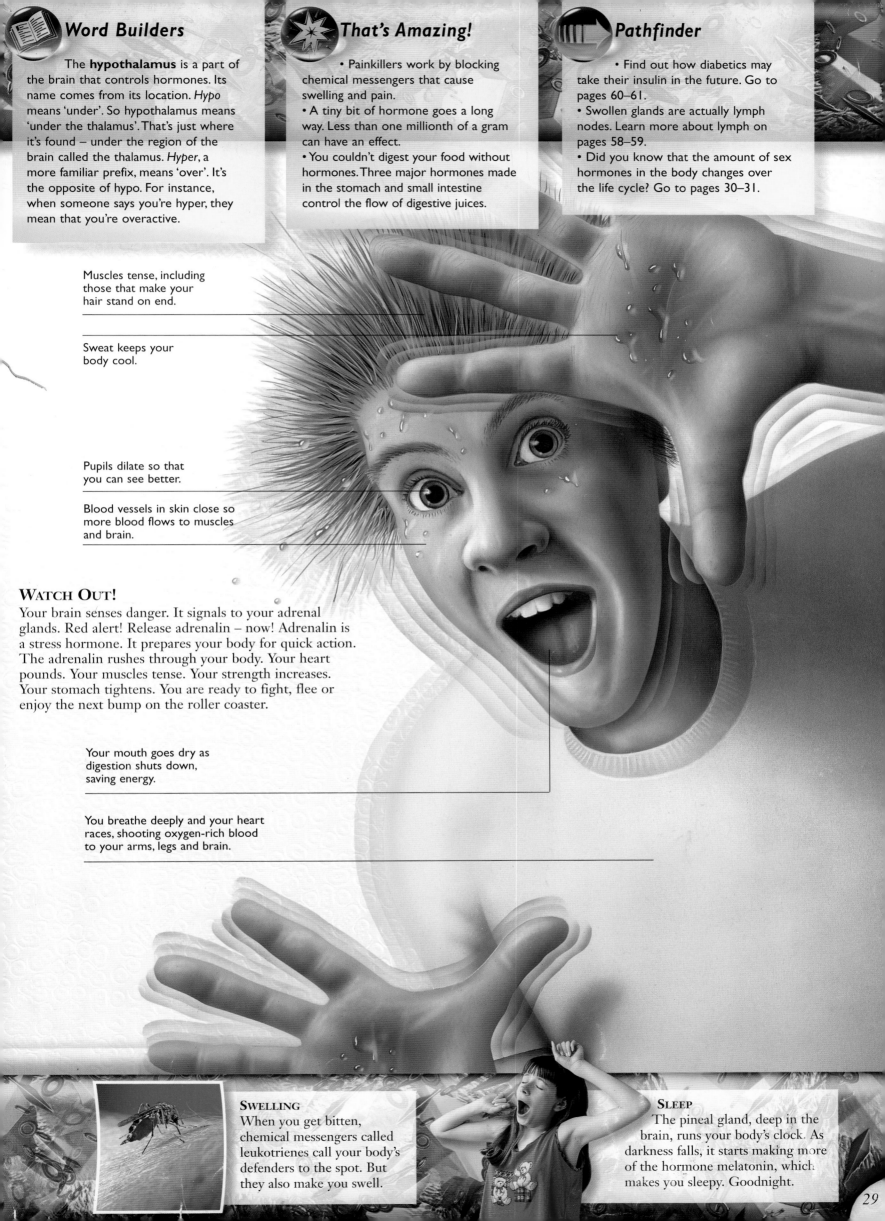

Word Builders

The **hypothalamus** is a part of the brain that controls hormones. Its name comes from its location. *Hypo* means 'under'. So hypothalamus means 'under the thalamus'. That's just where it's found – under the region of the brain called the thalamus. *Hyper*, a more familiar prefix, means 'over'. It's the opposite of hypo. For instance, when someone says you're hyper, they mean that you're overactive.

That's Amazing!

• Painkillers work by blocking chemical messengers that cause swelling and pain.
• A tiny bit of hormone goes a long way. Less than one millionth of a gram can have an effect.
• You couldn't digest your food without hormones. Three major hormones made in the stomach and small intestine control the flow of digestive juices.

Pathfinder

• Find out how diabetics may take their insulin in the future. Go to pages 60–61.
• Swollen glands are actually lymph nodes. Learn more about lymph on pages 58–59.
• Did you know that the amount of sex hormones in the body changes over the life cycle? Go to pages 30–31.

Muscles tense, including those that make your hair stand on end.

Sweat keeps your body cool.

Pupils dilate so that you can see better.

Blood vessels in skin close so more blood flows to muscles and brain.

WATCH OUT!

Your brain senses danger. It signals to your adrenal glands. Red alert! Release adrenalin – now! Adrenalin is a stress hormone. It prepares your body for quick action. The adrenalin rushes through your body. Your heart pounds. Your muscles tense. Your strength increases. Your stomach tightens. You are ready to fight, flee or enjoy the next bump on the roller coaster.

Your mouth goes dry as digestion shuts down, saving energy.

You breathe deeply and your heart races, shooting oxygen-rich blood to your arms, legs and brain.

SWELLING
When you get bitten, chemical messengers called leukotrienes call your body's defenders to the spot. But they also make you swell.

SLEEP
The pineal gland, deep in the brain, runs your body's clock. As darkness falls, it starts making more of the hormone melatonin, which makes you sleepy. Goodnight.

The Cycle of Life

HAVE YOU SEEN a photo of your mother or your father at your age? It's hard to imagine that they were once that young. It's even harder to imagine that one day you will be as old as they are now. Yet you will. Life's stages unfold for us all.

Look at how far you've come already. When you were born, your foot was no longer than your mother's thumb. Your fist was no bigger than your father's nose. A year or so later you could walk. You could play with your toys, find a crayon and scribble, but you could not yet draw, or talk or catch a ball. These accomplishments awaited a later stage of childhood.

As tiny as you were, the instructions for your growth were inside you already. They were encoded in your genes. Genes direct the growth of cells and the flow of hormones that bring each human life from conception to death. Along the way, each person passes through known stages. These stages, the life cycle, are the same for everyone. Not everyone lives them with the same health and vigour. The choices you make and the experiences you have influence how you grow and age. What happens when the cycle ends? That's a mystery to us all.

CYCLING ON

Our bodies change throughout the life cycle. When we're young, we see that change in outgrown jeans and T-shirts. The changes are less obvious in early adulthood. Over time, our cells become less efficient. Levels of hormones and brain chemicals drop. We age. We die. Death is sad for the person, but it is necessary. Earth would be too crowded if we lived for ever.

HANDS ON
My Family/Myself

You can trace the cycle of life within your own family by making a photographic time line. Can you find pictures of your relatives as babies? Or when they left school or got married? Look at how each person has changed, then talk to your relatives about the changes they've experienced. How did they feel about those changes? What do they do to stay healthy? Your family can help you understand the stages that await you.

Life span means the amount of time between birth and death. Scientists believe that the maximum life span for humans is 120 years. The oldest person on record died at 122. The average is much shorter, however. A child born in the U.S.A. today can expect to live to be about 76.

• We need less sleep as we get older. A newborn baby sleeps for about 20 hours a day. An 80-year-old may sleep as little as five hours a day.
• You grow more during the first year of life than at any other time.

• You can't control your bladder when you are a baby. Learn why on pages 50–51.
• See pages 34–35 to find out what causes your skin to wrinkle as you age.
• Will scientists be able to make humans live longer? Find out on pages 60–61.

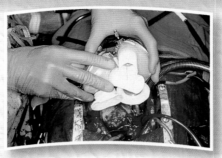

LIFE PRESERVERS

Science can help life at both ends of the life cycle. Doctors can combine egg and sperm outside the womb, creating a life that otherwise would not have been. They are also able to replace damaged body parts with new ones, such as this plastic heart valve.

MAKING A DIFFERENCE

Identical twins, such as these boys, have identical genes. These genes will influence their growth in many ways. They may influence how tall the boys become, when they reach puberty and even how long they live. Some diseases, such as heart disease, run in the family. So does long life. Genes aren't everything, however. Healthy habits help people avoid disease and live longer. One of these twins may outlive his brother if he takes better care of his mental and physical health. People often live longer when they are close to others, have a positive outlook on life and keep their minds active.

THE GROWTH FILES

The truth is out there. You're going to grow up. How will it happen? When will it happen? Read on.

COMING OF AGE

Girls become women and boys become men because of sex hormones. At around age 10 or 11 in girls and 12 or 13 in boys, sex hormones start flowing. Girls develop breasts and broader hips. They begin to menstruate. Boys' voices deepen. They grow facial hair. This stage of development is called puberty. By the end of it, both males and females are able to have children.

GROWING UP

Growth hormone brings you to your full height. It strengthens your muscles and bones. Your body makes growth hormone throughout life, but it makes less as you get older.

The Framework

WHAT HAS 206 BONES, more than 650 muscles and enough skin to cover a small dining-room table? Why, your body of course. Skin, muscles and bones give your body its shape and appearance. But that's not all they do. Skin protects you. Muscles move you. Bones shelter the soft inner parts of your body. How does each work? Read on.

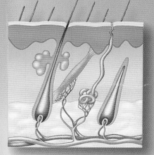

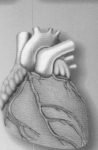

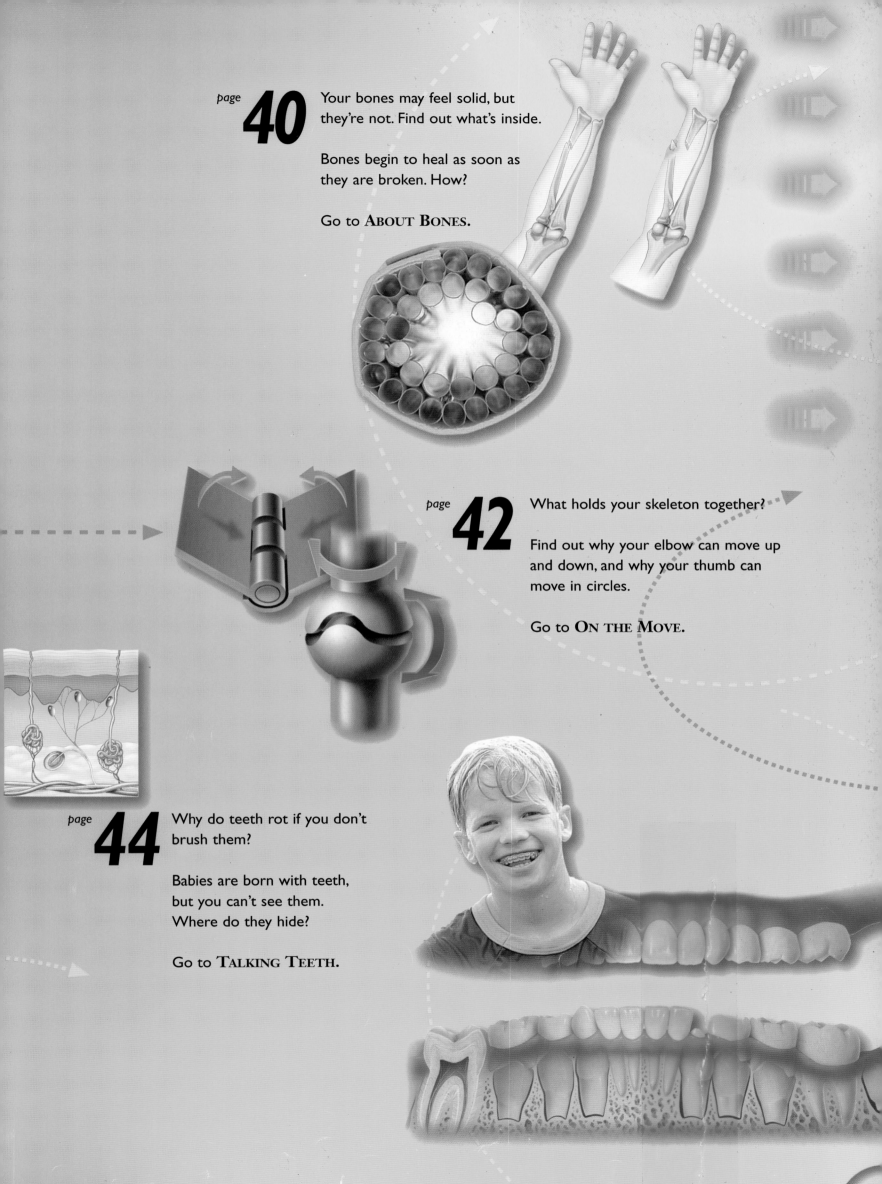

Skin Deep

TAKE A LOOK at your hand. In three weeks, the skin you see will be dust. A new batch will have grown to take its place. Your skin constantly renews itself. It must. You shed some each time you wash, dress, run, walk, scratch, clap or turn over in bed. Even tickling takes its toll. Skin is tough because it's built to take the abuse.

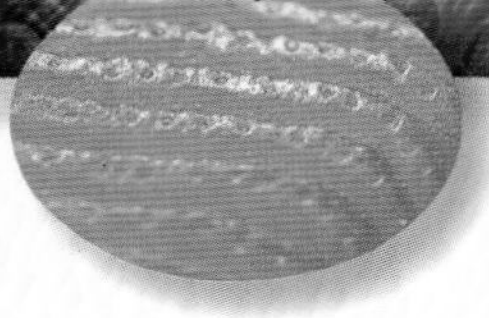

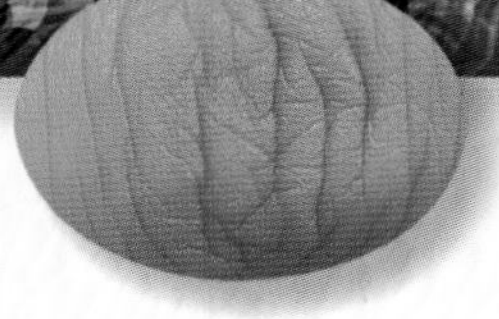

Skin is your body's largest organ. Its main job is to keep good stuff in and bad stuff out. It is both waterproof and germproof. Skin also controls body temperature and absorbs the sunlight you need to make vitamin D, which is essential for strong bones and teeth. Of course, skin also gives you your sense of touch.

You feel what you touch because skin is rich in nerve endings. The nerve endings are your body's alarm system. They sense hot and cold, pressure and pain. They tell you that the bath is too hot or that a bee has just attacked. They crowd your fingers, toes and lips – the parts of your body you use to test the safety of the world. Touch also brings you pleasure, which is vital for survival, as well. Babies who aren't held and stroked can suffer severe emotional damage. Skin's benefits are more than skin deep.

HANDS ON
Skin's Paintbrush

Your skin gets its colour from melanin. This pigment is made in special skin cells. Other skin cells then absorb it. The more melanin you have, the darker your skin. People from hot places, such as Africa, need more melanin. It soaks up the Sun's harmful rays, protecting the skin's lower layers.

You can see melanin at work in your own skin. Wear a bandage for a few days. When you remove it, you'll see a change in your skin colour. Try this in different seasons.

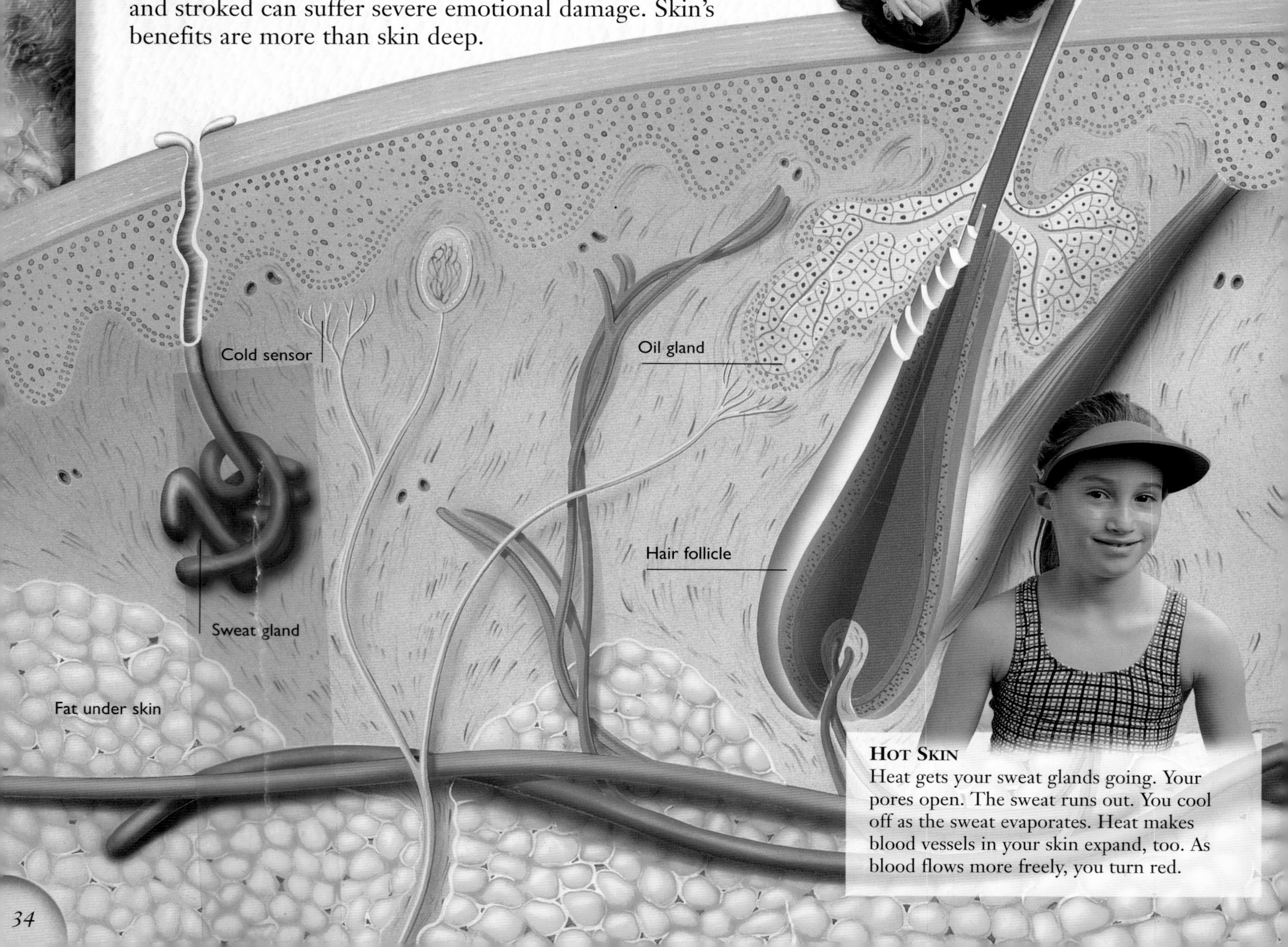

Cold sensor

Oil gland

Hair follicle

Sweat gland

Fat under skin

HOT SKIN
Heat gets your sweat glands going. Your pores open. The sweat runs out. You cool off as the sweat evaporates. Heat makes blood vessels in your skin expand, too. As blood flows more freely, you turn red.

Word Builders

Some people have no colour in their skin, eyes or hair. They are called **albinos**, from the Latin word *albus*, which means 'white'. Their body doesn't make melanin, the pigment that colours skin. Scar tissue doesn't have melanin, either. It is made of collagen, not skin cells. Sometimes, one area of skin has more melanin than another. The result is freckles or a mole.

That's Amazing!

• During your life, you'll shed about 47.6 kilograms (105 lb) of skin.
• Humans are the only animals that blush with emotion. Anger or embarrassment can turn your cheeks red.
• The ridges and valleys of your fingertips help you get a good grip. They are unique. Not even identical twins share the same fingerprints.

Pathfinder

• As we age, the skin's springy fibres become stiff. That's why we wrinkle. Pages 30–31 tell more about ageing.
• A substance called keratin makes skin, hair and nails tough. Find out more on pages 36–37.
• What do your skin and skeleton have in common? The answer is on pages 40–41.

Spot City

Spots are proof that you can have too much of a good thing. Glands in your skin make an oily substance called sebum. Sebum helps keep skin moist. Too much of it can clog pores, causing spots.

Layer upon Layer

Your skin is constructed like an iced cake. The 'cake', the skin's thick lower layer, is the dermis. The thin 'icing' is the epidermis. The epidermis constantly makes new skin cells. They form at its base and push their way to the top. Along the way, they become flat and tough. By the time they reach the surface, they're dead. The dermis is made mainly of collagen, the protein that gives skin its spring. Hair shafts, sweat glands, oil glands and nerve endings fill this layer, too. So do blood vessels that nourish the epidermis.

INSIDE STORY

Healing Skin

Skin repairs itself, but some burns and wounds are so severe the skin can't make new cells fast enough. In these cases, doctors can sometimes take skin from another part of a patient's body to cover the wound. They can also use artificial skin made from shark cartilage, but the body may reject this. Now, though, they may have a better choice. Scientists can grow human skin in a laboratory. The patient's body accepts this artificial skin as its own.

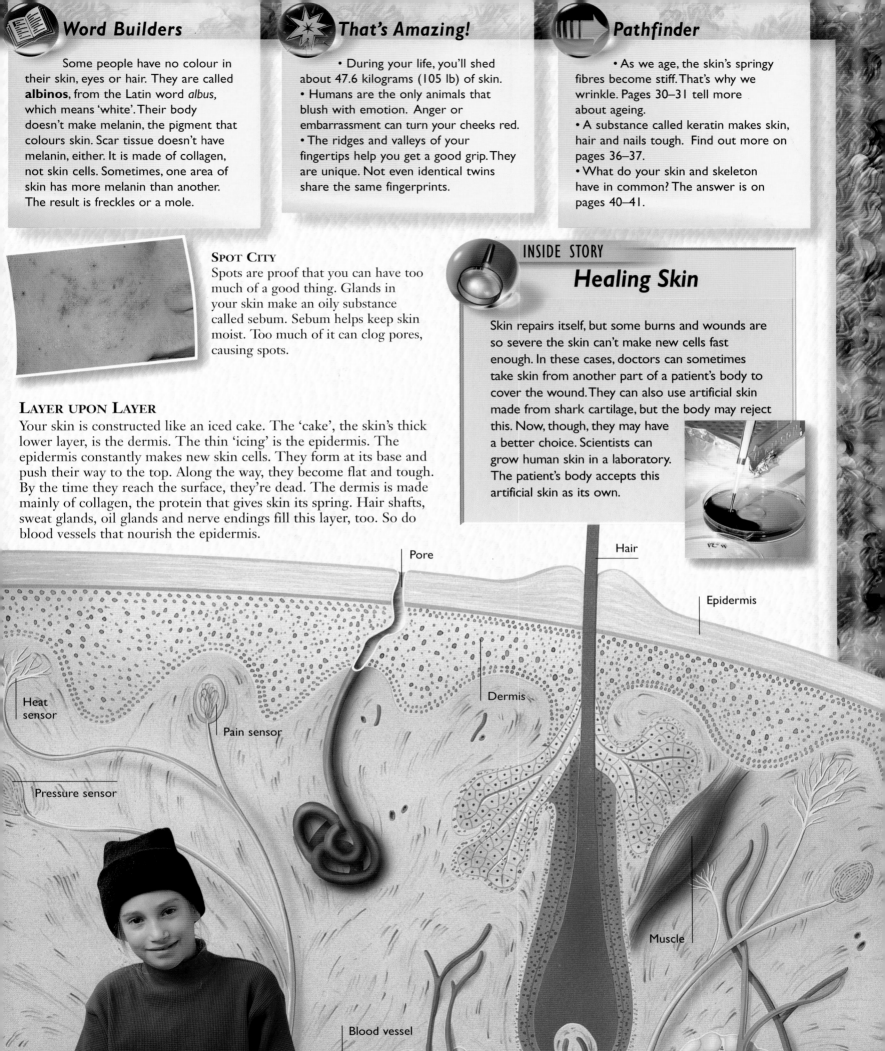

Cold Skin

When you're cold, blood vessels in your skin contract to trap heat. You lose colour. Tiny muscles attached to hair follicles contract to keep warm air from escaping, too. The result? Goose-pimples.

 *Straight hair*

 *Wavy hair*

Curly hair

Hair and Nails

RUN YOUR FINGERS gently over your cheek. Do you feel the soft, downy hairs? Now check your stomach or thigh. Can you feel the hairs there, too? Hair covers almost all of your skin. The major exceptions are your lips, palms and the soles of your feet. What does all this hair do? Let's take it from the top.

The thick mane on your head is a natural sunscreen for your scalp. It absorbs sweat, conserves heat in winter and softens the occasional blow. Hairs in your nose and ears trap germs. Eyelashes blink away dust. What's more, all hairs are tiny sense organs. Bend one and it triggers a nearby nerve, enhancing your sense of touch.

Although they don't look it, your nails have a lot in common with your hair. Both are dead and toughened with keratin, a protein also found in skin. Like some of your hair, nails protect you by shielding sensitive skin. Have you ever banged a finger or toe? Imagine how that would feel without a nail.

Genes determine the strength and shape of your nails. They also dictate whether you have curly blonde tresses or straight black ones. Fashion often overrules nature. Since early times, humans have changed their hair and nails to express their personality and to attract mates. Have you ever changed yours?

HEAD TO TOE
Your hair grows about 12.7 centimetres (5 in) a year, but every two to five years, each follicle takes a rest. It makes no new hair cells for about three months, then starts again.

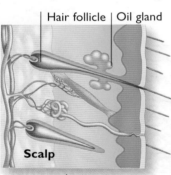

Hair follicle | Oil gland

Scalp

Sweat glands

Armpit

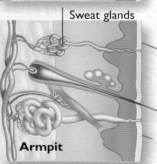

Pain and pressure sensors

Sole of foot

HOW HAIR GROWS
The base of each follicle is shaped like a bulb. Here, new hair cells form constantly. As these new cells press their way up, they drive older, dead cells to the surface. Glands on the side of the follicle coat the growing hair with an oil. This keeps it soft and flexible. Your hair is thicker in some places than others because you have more follicles there. Some places, such as the sole of your foot, have no follicles at all.

HANDS ON
How Fast Do Your Nails Grow?

Your nails never stop growing, but they grow more slowly than hair. Fingernails grow about 3.8 centimetres (1.5 in) a year. Toenails are twice as slow. Just how fast do your nails grow? Find out.

❶ Measure the length of your nails from base to tip once a week. Measure each fingernail and toenail. Ask a parent to do the same.

❷ Plot the results on a growth chart.

What differences can you see? How much faster do your fingernails grow than your toenails? Do the nails on one hand grow faster than those on the other? Whose grow fastest?

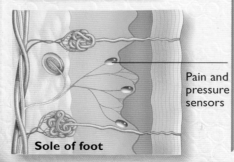

Word Builders

A **follicle** is the tiny pouch deep in your skin from which a hair grows. The word comes from the Latin *folliculus*, which means 'little bag'. Your follicles influence whether your hair is coarse or fine, curly or straight. The smaller the follicles, the finer the hair. If cells form evenly in the base of the follicle, hair is straight. If they form unevenly, hair is curly.

That's Amazing!

• You shed 50–100 hairs a day.
• By four months, a fine coat of hair covers the foetus. It is called lanugo. Many babies still have this hair at birth.
• Nails grow fastest during early adulthood. Growth is slowest during infancy and old age.
• Tiny mites can live in the follicles of your eyelashes. They feed on the oils in the skin.

Pathfinder

• Hairs in your ear canal trap dust and germs. What else keeps debris out of your ears? Find out on pages 22–23.
• Some hair follicles are present at birth but don't become active until puberty. Learn about puberty on pages 30–31.
• Goose-pimples are caused by contractions of the tiny muscles around each hair. For more on muscles, go to pages 38–39.

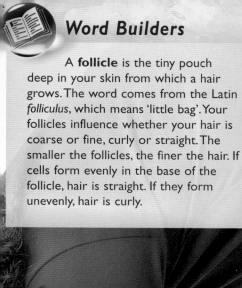

HAIR COLOUR

Hair gets its colour from melanin, the same pigment that colours skin. As people age, their follicles stop making melanin. Hair turns white or grey.

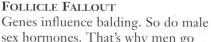

FOLLICLE FALLOUT

Genes influence balding. So do male sex hormones. That's why men go bald more often than women. Hair loss in women is usually less noticeable than in men. Women's hair generally thins all over, so most don't get bald spots.

NAILS TELL TALES

Nails grow from under the skin at their base. The area that makes new nail cells is called the matrix. The skin that covers and protects it is the cuticle. Even small changes in the shape and colour of your nails can signal trouble. Liver disease turns the skin under the nail yellow, for instance. Heart disease can make it blue.

The matrix produces new nail cells.

The nail plate is the visible nail.

The cuticle covers and protects the matrix.

The nail plate covers the nail bed.

The white half circle is the lunule.

NASTY NAILS

Heart or lung disease can cause fingers to swell, which makes the nail bulge.

Frequent use of chemicals, such as detergents and hair dyes, can cause nails to curve.

A bang can cause harmless white spots in the nail. White spots *under* the nail may be from a fungus.

Illness can cause nails to grow poorly. The ridges disappear as the nail grows out.

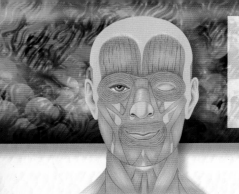

Frown   *Surprise*   *Smile*

Mighty Muscles

HAS ANYONE EVER told you not to move a muscle? It's impossible to do. You can decide not to tap your foot or wiggle your finger, but your heart and stomach are muscles, too, and you can't control them.

Muscles are your body's power stations. They convert energy into pulling power. The ones you can control are skeletal muscles. You have about 650 of these. They attach to your bones with tough ropes of tissue called tendons. Skeletal muscles work in pairs to move you. One contracts, or tightens, to pull on a bone. At the same time, its sister muscle relaxes. Then the sister muscle contracts and the first one relaxes. The bone moves back. Whether you're jumping or playing a guitar, the mechanism is the same.

The muscles you can't control are called smooth muscle because they look smooth under the microscope. Smooth muscle forms the walls of your blood vessels and intestines. It lets your stomach contract to process food. Your most powerful muscle is neither smooth nor skeletal. It's called cardiac muscle. What is it? Your heart.

Blood vessels and nerves feed all your muscles. The blood vessels supply fuel and oxygen. Nerves direct the muscles' actions. Think about this as you use your eye muscles to read on.

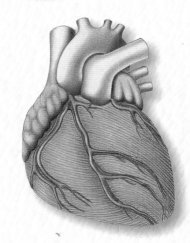

ONE TOUGH MUSCLE
Your tireless heart beats more than 4,500 times each hour. Its muscle is unique. The cells look striped, like skeletal muscle, but you can't control it.

MUSCLE MAPS
Have you used your gluteus maximus lately? You have if you've stood up. How about your rectus abdominus? It gets a workout every time you cough. Look at the muscle maps below to find these and other major muscles. The maps can't show all your muscles. Each hand alone has 37. You even have muscles inside your ears to move tiny ear bones. One of these is the stapedius, your smallest muscle. It looks like a wisp of cotton.

HANDS ON
Tricky Muscles

❶ A tendon attaches each finger to the muscles in your forearm. Place your hand as shown in the picture. Try to lift each of the extended fingers. Can't move your ring finger? That's because its tendon connects with the middle finger's tendon. This limits your ability to move the finger on its own.

❷ While your friend holds it down, try to raise your arm for 30 seconds. What happens when your friend lets go? Your muscle 'remembers' that you were trying to lift it.

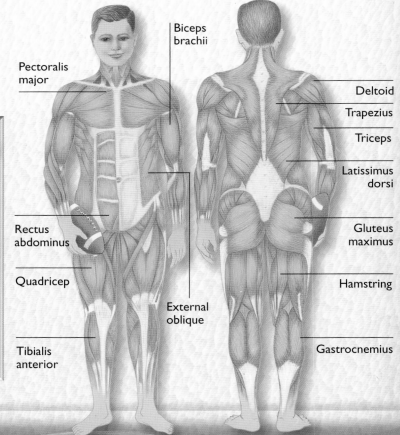

Pectoralis major
Biceps brachii
Rectus abdominus
Quadricep
Tibialis anterior
External oblique
Deltoid
Trapezius
Triceps
Latissimus dorsi
Gluteus maximus
Hamstring
Gastrocnemius

Muscle   Muscle cell bundle

GETTING DOWN TO DETAIL
Bundles of muscle cells make up each of your muscles. Each muscle cell is, in turn, made up of smaller bundles of fibres called myofibrils. *Myo* means 'muscle'. Within each myofibril, thin strands of protein surround thick ones. When a muscle contracts, the thick strands pull the thin ones closer together. The cell, and the muscle, shortens. You flex your arm.

Word Builders

When you and your brother fight, you are antagonists. You're enemies. Muscles are called **antagonists** when they work together. This is because they have opposite actions. When one contracts, the other relaxes. **Contract** means 'to draw together', or shorten.

That's Amazing!

• Your muscle cells produce enough heat every day to boil almost 1 litre (2 pt) of water for an hour.
• When you shiver, your muscles contract involuntarily. This releases energy that keeps your body warm.
• You use your muscles to stand still. Try it. Stand as still as you can. Gravity will make you sway, but your muscles will pull you straight again.

Pathfinder

• Your eye muscles are the most active in the body. To find out more, go to pages 20–21.
• Muscles move bones, but bones also protect muscles. To bone up on bones, turn to pages 40–41.
• Muscle cells are packed with mitochondria, which produce all that muscle energy. Learn more about cells on pages 10–11.

MUSCLE POWER

Muscles you don't use lose strength and size. Those you use a great deal grow strong and big. The repeated stress of swinging a bat or lifting weights, for instance, causes the muscle fibres to thicken. Body builders do special exercises to develop all of their major muscles. You don't have to look like a body builder to be strong. Regular exercise will keep your muscles fit.

Muscle cell

Myofibril

Protein strands

Protein strands when muscle is relaxed

Protein strands when muscle is contracted

Bone-bending Fashions

Chinese women used to have their feet broken and bound.

Some women from Burma wore neck rings that stretched vertebrae.

Western women wore corsets that squashed lower ribs.

About Bones

YOUR BONES ARE so strong that just a small piece of one can support the weight of an elephant. A lot of bone supports *your* weight and protects your delicate insides. Your skull bones form a natural helmet for your brain. Ribs create a cage around your heart, liver and lungs. The pelvis cradles your lower organs. The vertebrae of your spine encircle your spinal cord. While your bones are standing guard, they are also making your blood cells and storing minerals for the body's use.

Bone has three busy layers. A thin outer layer called the periosteum wraps around a hard shell called compact bone. Compact bone looks solid, but it isn't. The bone grows in circles around hollow canals. Blood vessels in these canals deliver food and oxygen to the bone cells. Beneath the shell of compact bone is a spongy web of minerals and marrow. The bone marrow is where blood cells are made.

Throughout life, bone makes and remakes itself. One type of bone cell constantly breaks old bone down while another builds new bone up. Hormones play a role in this process but so do your activities. As you move around each day, the push of gravity and the pull of muscles stimulate new bone growth. Strong muscles make strong bones.

HANDS ON

Build a Bone

Bone is so hard that surgeons must cut it with a saw. It is also light because of air pockets in the core. Make a model bone using stiff paper, tape, scissors and drinking straws. Then test its strength.

❶ Cut a piece of stiff paper 14 centimetres (5.5 in) wide and the length of a straw.

❷ Using double-sided tape, line the paper with two layers of straws. Roll the paper into a tube with straws on the inside. Tape it firmly shut with sticky tape.

❸ Stand your 'bone' upright on a table. Now press hard with your hands or a book. How strong is your bone?

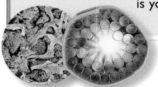

Real bone   Straw bone

SEE THROUGH ME

You have twice as many bones as a giraffe – and as most other mammals. The reason is because you have hands and feet. Together, they contain more than half of your 206 bones. That's why they are so flexible. Bones tell a lot about a person. Even thousands of years after death, they reveal secrets of a person's health, lifestyle, height and sex.

INSIDE STORY

A Glow in the Dark

On 8 November, 1895, German scientist Wilhelm Roentgen was working with electricity when he discovered a new kind of light. It passed through paper, books and tin. It made skin invisible and lit up the bones beneath. Roentgen stayed in his lab for the next two months, experimenting with this light he called an 'X-ray'. He found that he could take photos with X-rays, capturing images of the inside of the body. Within months, doctors around the world were using X-rays to diagnose broken bones and other problems.

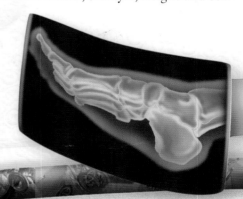

BROKEN BONES

Sticks and stones don't usually break bones, but falls and accidents do. A break in a bone is called a fracture. Doctors X-ray a fracture to see the amount and type of damage. Then they set the bone, making sure the broken pieces line up. The bone would heal without help, but it might not grow straight and strong. A cast keeps the bone still and in place while it heals.

BAD BREAKS

In a simple fracture, the bone breaks but the skin doesn't. In a compound fracture, the bone pierces the skin. This can be a more serious injury because germs can enter and infect the fractured bone.

Word Builders

- Doctors don't know whether bones cause **growing pains**, but they do know that growing doesn't. Children grow most during their first three years and in their teens, but they don't get growing pains then.
- Your **funny bone** is misnamed, too. It's really a nerve, not a bone. Its name comes from the nearby upper arm bone, the humerus. Get it?

That's Amazing!

- Bone is the second-hardest substance in your body. Only tooth enamel is harder.
- You don't need a cast for a broken rib. Your chest muscles hold it in place.
- Your bones hold 98 per cent of the body's calcium supply. Your body uses these supplies if you don't get enough calcium in your diet. Over time, this can weaken bones.

Pathfinder

- Your bones make your blood cells. Find out more on pages 56–57.
- Learn how bones hold together to form your skeleton. Go to pages 42–43.
- Bone isn't the only body tissue that renews itself all the time. Skin does, too. Find out more on pages 34–35.

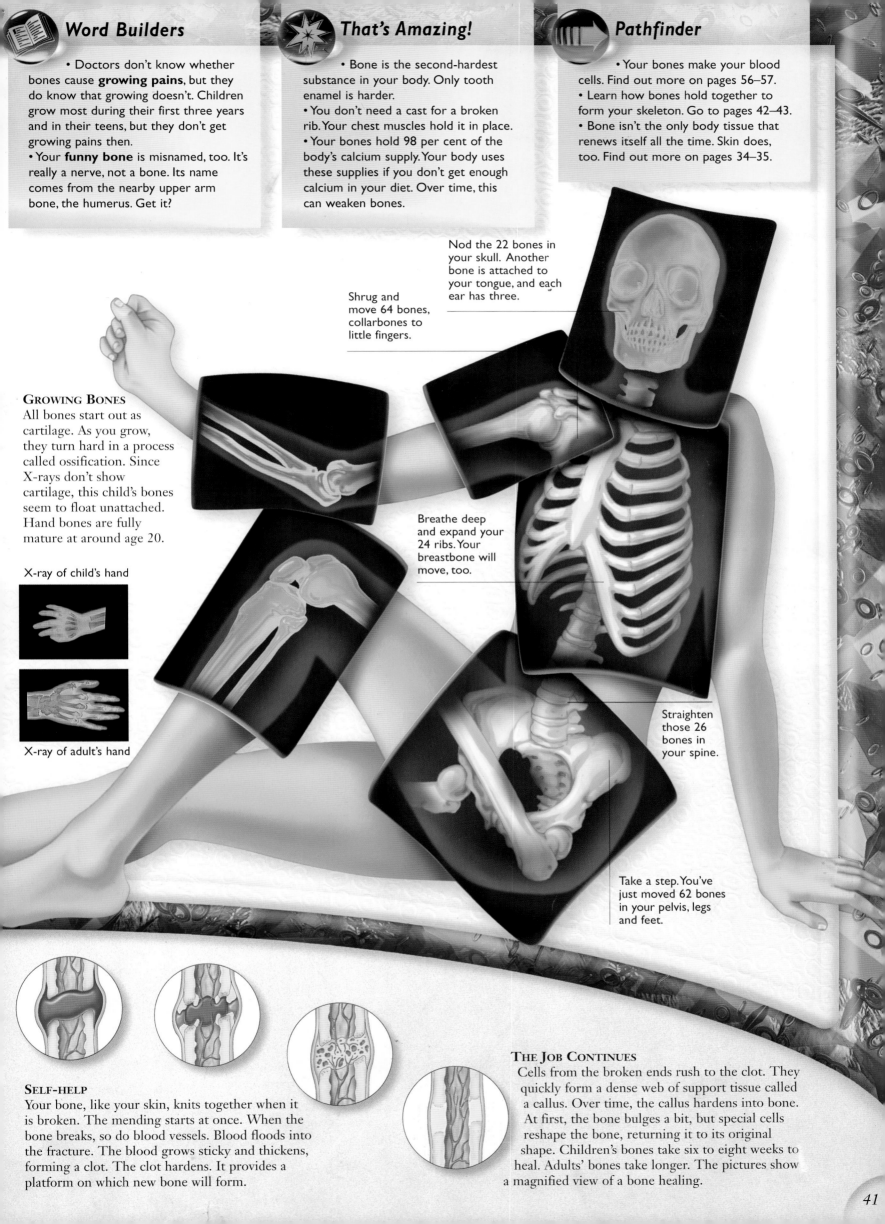

Nod the 22 bones in your skull. Another bone is attached to your tongue, and each ear has three.

Shrug and move 64 bones, collarbones to little fingers.

GROWING BONES
All bones start out as cartilage. As you grow, they turn hard in a process called ossification. Since X-rays don't show cartilage, this child's bones seem to float unattached. Hand bones are fully mature at around age 20.

X-ray of child's hand

X-ray of adult's hand

Breathe deep and expand your 24 ribs. Your breastbone will move, too.

Straighten those 26 bones in your spine.

Take a step. You've just moved 62 bones in your pelvis, legs and feet.

SELF-HELP
Your bone, like your skin, knits together when it is broken. The mending starts at once. When the bone breaks, so do blood vessels. Blood floods into the fracture. The blood grows sticky and thickens, forming a clot. The clot hardens. It provides a platform on which new bone will form.

THE JOB CONTINUES
Cells from the broken ends rush to the clot. They quickly form a dense web of support tissue called a callus. Over time, the callus hardens into bone. At first, the bone bulges a bit, but special cells reshape the bone, returning it to its original shape. Children's bones take six to eight weeks to heal. Adults' bones take longer. The pictures show a magnified view of a bone healing.

Arm straight   *Bicep muscle relaxed*   *Arm bent*   *Bicep muscle contracted*

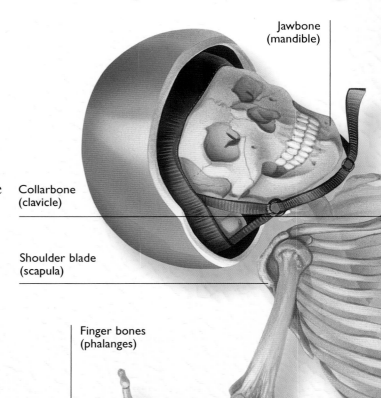

Jawbone (mandible)

Collarbone (clavicle)

Shoulder blade (scapula)

Finger bones (phalanges)

Wrist bones (carpals)

On the Move

TRY A FRANKENSTEIN walk. Hold your legs stiff and take a few steps. Now try running that way. You can't get very far or go very fast. What if your arm was a single bone? Could you scratch your back or bring an ice-cream cone to your mouth? Imagine a spine as straight and stiff as a ruler. You couldn't look over your shoulder or touch your toes, let alone ride a skateboard.

Your skeleton is cleverly constructed. It lets you bend, twist and twirl. It protects your insides and supports as much as five times its own weight in muscles and organs. This sturdy frame is shaped differently in men and women. A woman's wide pelvis allows room for a baby to grow. A man's broad shoulder bones support his heavier muscles.

Bones can't bend, but you need to and because of joints you can. A joint is where two bones meet. Your joints let bones move only in certain directions and prevent them from moving the wrong way. Some joints let bones move only up and down, while others let them swivel. Joints wouldn't work, however, without muscles. Tendons anchor muscle to bone. When the muscle contracts, it moves the bone in the joint. Your knees bend. Your arms extend for balance. You ride that skateboard.

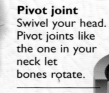

HANDS ON
Straight Talk About Spines

Your spine is your body's central support. It transfers the weight of your upper body to your pelvis and legs. When you stand straight, your weight is evenly distributed along your spine. When you slouch, the weight strains one part of your spine.

❶ Be aware of your body. Balance a book on your head and walk. Your head is high and your shoulders are slightly back. This is back-healthy posture.

❷ Keep your spine straight and your knees bent when you lift things. That way, your strong legs — not your spine — will absorb the extra load.

Pivot joint
Swivel your head. Pivot joints like the one in your neck let bones rotate.

JOINT ACTION
The shape of a joint determines how — and if — bones move. Some joints in your skull allow no movement. These 'suture' joints hold bones snug to protect the brain. Other joints, such as those in your spine, let bones move just a bit. The tiny movements of your 24 vertebrae add up to a flexible spine, however. Touch your toes, then read on to learn about other joints.

42

Word Builders

Collagen is your body's glue. Its name comes from the ancient Greek *kolla*, which means 'glue', and *gen*, which means 'something that causes'. Collagen is the main ingredient in the special tissues that hold your body together. These are called connective tissues. They are found throughout your body. Ligaments and tendons are connective tissues. So, too, are your bones, which form the frame that supports the rest of you.

That's Amazing!

• No one is really double-jointed. Some people simply have flexible ligaments.
• Sensors in your joints tell your brain if the joint is bent. Your brain combines this information about your movement and position with messages from your senses to help you keep your balance.

Pathfinder

• What joints are the most active in the body? Find out on pages 44–45.
• Cartilage doesn't naturally replace itself, but scientists may be able to make it grow. Find out how on pages 60–61.
• Your skeleton protects your brain and spinal cord – the central nervous system. Learn about the nervous system on pages 14–15.

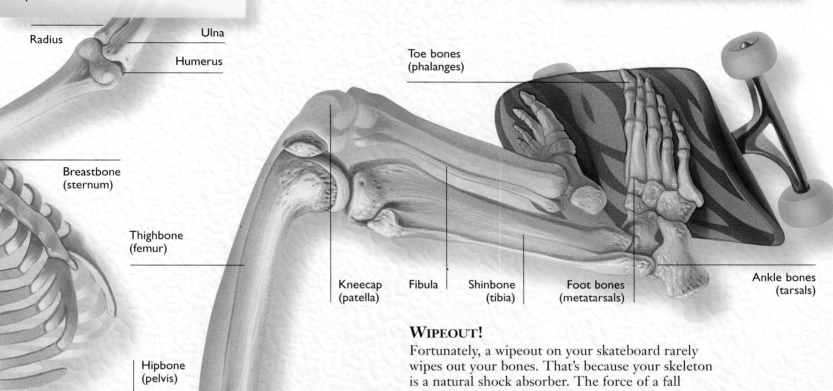

Radius
Ulna
Humerus
Breastbone (sternum)
Thighbone (femur)
Hipbone (pelvis)
Tailbone (coccyx)
Toe bones (phalanges)
Kneecap (patella)
Fibula
Shinbone (tibia)
Foot bones (metatarsals)
Ankle bones (tarsals)

WIPEOUT!

Fortunately, a wipeout on your skateboard rarely wipes out your bones. That's because your skeleton is a natural shock absorber. The force of a fall radiates through the bone to the joint. There, cartilage and fluid absorb some of the shock. A bent elbow or knee, or the spring-like curve of the spine, also softens the blow. Bones can still break, of course, especially if hit straight on.

Saddle joint
Thumbs up! A saddle joint, like the one in your thumb, gives movement two ways – up and down and across.

Ball-and-socket joint
Swing your arms. Ball-and-socket joints in your shoulders and hips let bones move all around.

Hinge joint
Flex your arm. Thanks to a hinge joint, your elbow bends up and down. Find other hinge joints.

INSIDE STORY

Where Bones Meet

Joints that move are built for a lifetime of action, with padding to protect bones from wearing out. Smooth cartilage coats the ends of each bone. Slippery synovial fluid moistens the joint and lessens friction. Tough, flexible ligaments bind the joint together and keep it from moving too much. In some joints, such as those of the spine, cushiony discs of cartilage separate the bones. All these parts work together. It's truly a joint effort.

Ligaments
Cartilage
Fluid

Talking Teeth

TAP YOUR FRONT teeth. You've just touched the hardest substance in your body. Your teeth are built to last. Over an average life, they will tear, chomp, grind and chew some 30,000 tonnes of food. That's about 240 million hamburgers. Your chomping, grinding teeth begin the process of digestion, but that's not all they do. Teeth are a rigid gate, protecting the rest of your mouth from blows. They help shape speech from the sounds your vocal cords produce. They also contribute to appearance, of course. Imagine a smile without any teeth.

Your teeth started forming before you were born. All 20 baby teeth and many of your adult teeth were present as tiny buds under the gums. They grew slowly, pushing into the open as your jaw developed. They are growing still. A child's jaw isn't big enough for adult teeth, which is why you get two sets.

Whether a tooth belongs to a baby or an adult, it is made of hard, shock-absorbing dentin. A layer of even harder enamel protects the dentin above the gum. Bone-like cementum covers the root. Nerves and blood vessels run through the tooth's soft core, the pulp. A sling of ligaments connects each tooth to your bony jaw. Together, ligaments and bone hold your teeth firmly in place. That should give you something to smile about.

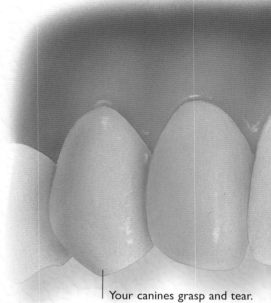

Your canines grasp and tear.

IN THE PINK
Gums cover and protect the bone that anchors teeth. If infected, the gums pull away from the teeth. Germs can move in and attack bone, loosening teeth. You can tell that gums are healthy when they are pink.

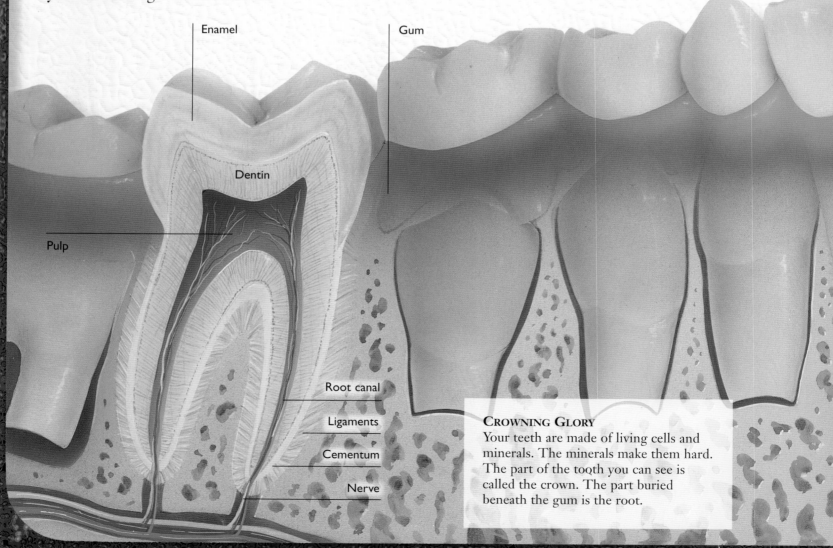

Enamel

Gum

Dentin

Pulp

Root canal

Ligaments

Cementum

Nerve

CROWNING GLORY
Your teeth are made of living cells and minerals. The minerals make them hard. The part of the tooth you can see is called the crown. The part buried beneath the gum is the root.

A thin slime of bacteria, mucus and food debris constantly forms on teeth. It's called **plaque.** Brushing removes plaque. If plaque isn't removed, it hardens into tartar. The tartar can build up between the tooth and gum. This leaves pockets through which bacteria can reach and destroy bone. This condition is called gum disease, and it is the main reason people lose teeth.

• Tooth enamel is the second-hardest natural substance in the world. Only diamonds are harder.
• Saliva is a natural mouthwash. It kills bacteria. You produce enough saliva in your lifetime to fill a swimming pool.
• Your back teeth are shaped like shovels so that they can help move food into your mouth.

• Your teeth start the process of digestion. Find out how it ends on pages 48–49.
• Your jaw joints are the most active in the body. You use them every time you smile, yawn, chew or talk. Learn about other joints on pages 42–43.
• Without saliva, you couldn't taste your food. Find out why on pages 26–27.

INSIDE STORY

The Great Stain Mystery

These teeth were strange. They had stains as dark as chocolate. Stranger still, they had no decay. What was going on? A young dentist named Frederick McKay first asked this question in 1901. He had opened an office in Colorado Springs, Colorado, U.S.A. Many of his patients had this unusual staining. For 30 years, McKay tried to find out why. He finally found the answer in the water. The local water contained lots of a chemical called fluoride. When children drank the water, the fluoride stained their teeth, but it also protected them from decay. Only tiny amounts of fluoride are needed to protect teeth. Today, it's added to toothpaste, mouthwash and drinking water in many areas.

Bite in with those incisors.

CHOMP!

When you bite down on an apple, your top and bottom teeth should line up correctly. If they don't, it's hard to keep your teeth clean and healthy. You may also have trouble chewing or even speaking well. Braces can correct such problems.

THE TOOTH EATERS
Most bacteria will brush off your teeth, but some get trapped in tiny pits and grooves. These bacteria make acid that eats through the enamel and leads to tooth decay.

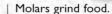
Premolars hold and crush food.

Molars grind food.

BRUSH THOSE TEETH
Baby teeth are good for more than money from the tooth fairy. They hold places for the adult teeth below. Without baby teeth as a guide, adult teeth would grow in crooked and crowded. So take good care of those baby whites.

Supplies and Demand

BEFORE YOU HAD fingers, toes, eyes or ears, you had a heart. It beat when you'd been in your mother's womb for just three weeks. It helped move life-giving oxygen and nutrients through your body. Before birth, these vital supplies came from your mother. Where do they come from now? What happens as your body uses them? What else moves through your blood? Turn the page.

page

54

Why does your heart beat faster when you run?

How is blood transported into every corner of your body?

Go to **HEART OF THE MATTER**.

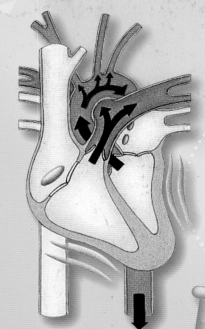

page

56

These cells are lifesavers (below left). Find out why.

What's in every drop of blood?

Go to **IT'S IN THE BLOOD**.

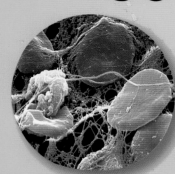

page

58

There's a war going on right now inside you. Read all about it.

Your body has more than 100 germ-fighting centres. Where are they? What are they?

Go to **PROTECTING US**.

page

60

Soon a potato might protect you from disease. How?

Will human beings look very different in the future? Will we live longer?

Go to **FUTURE US**.

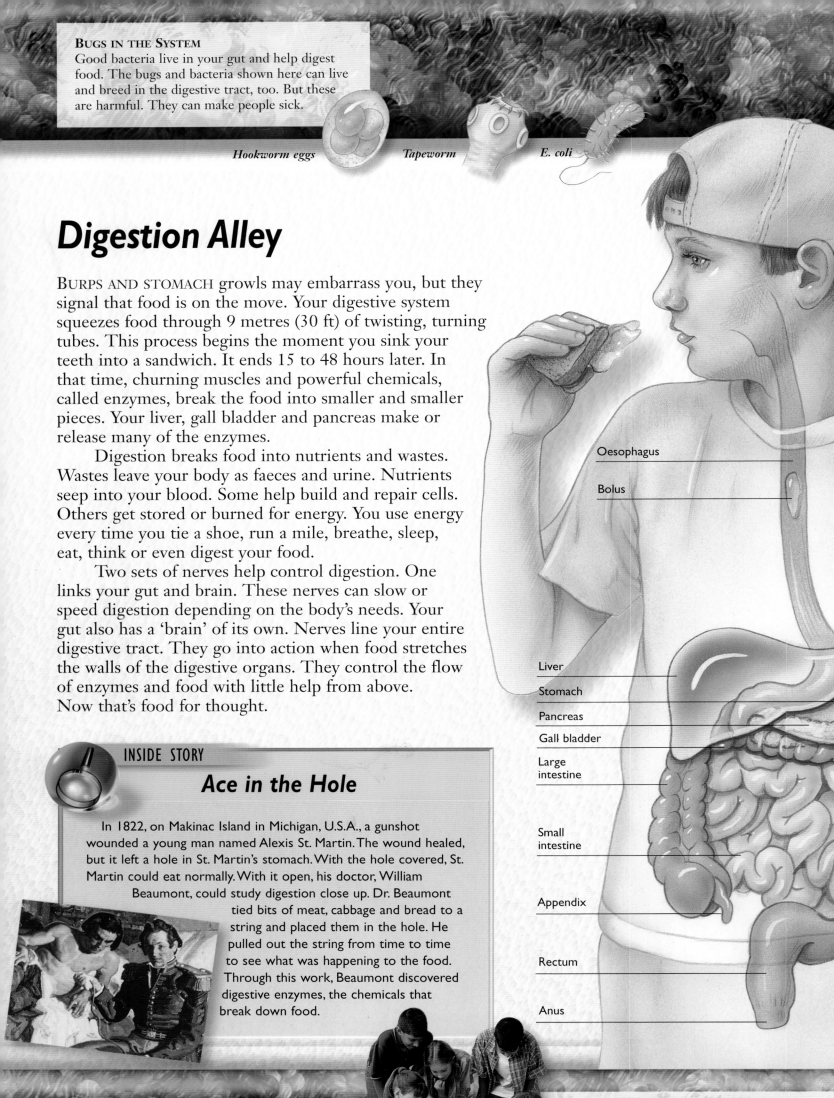

Hookworm eggs   *Tapeworm*   *E. coli*

Digestion Alley

BURPS AND STOMACH growls may embarrass you, but they signal that food is on the move. Your digestive system squeezes food through 9 metres (30 ft) of twisting, turning tubes. This process begins the moment you sink your teeth into a sandwich. It ends 15 to 48 hours later. In that time, churning muscles and powerful chemicals, called enzymes, break the food into smaller and smaller pieces. Your liver, gall bladder and pancreas make or release many of the enzymes.

Digestion breaks food into nutrients and wastes. Wastes leave your body as faeces and urine. Nutrients seep into your blood. Some help build and repair cells. Others get stored or burned for energy. You use energy every time you tie a shoe, run a mile, breathe, sleep, eat, think or even digest your food.

Two sets of nerves help control digestion. One links your gut and brain. These nerves can slow or speed digestion depending on the body's needs. Your gut also has a 'brain' of its own. Nerves line your entire digestive tract. They go into action when food stretches the walls of the digestive organs. They control the flow of enzymes and food with little help from above. Now that's food for thought.

Oesophagus

Bolus

Liver

Stomach

Pancreas

Gall bladder

Large intestine

Small intestine

Appendix

Rectum

Anus

INSIDE STORY

Ace in the Hole

In 1822, on Makinac Island in Michigan, U.S.A., a gunshot wounded a young man named Alexis St. Martin. The wound healed, but it left a hole in St. Martin's stomach. With the hole covered, St. Martin could eat normally. With it open, his doctor, William Beaumont, could study digestion close up. Dr. Beaumont tied bits of meat, cabbage and bread to a string and placed them in the hole. He pulled out the string from time to time to see what was happening to the food. Through this work, Beaumont discovered digestive enzymes, the chemicals that break down food.

ENERGY FROM FOOD
You need energy to read, to run – even to breathe. Digestion releases this energy from food. Your genes influence how quickly you burn the energy. So do the things you do. The more active you are, the more energy you use.

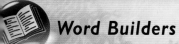

Word Builders

If you've ever washed a greasy pan with detergent, you know how your body digests fat. Your liver makes a 'detergent' called **bile,** which dissolves fats in the small intestine. Your gall bladder stores the bile.

That's Amazing!

• The wastes from a meal can take up to five days to leave your body.
• You don't use your appendix. This part of the large intestine may once have broken down fibres in our ancestors' leafy diet.

Pathfinder

• Your stomach makes its own hormones to aid digestion. Learn more on pages 28–29.
• Your large intestine rids the body of solid wastes. How do you get rid of liquid wastes? Find out on pages 50–51.
• Your liver is a multi-purpose organ. It makes sugar for energy, stores vitamins and minerals and cleans your blood. Learn more on pages 56–57.

FOOD PROCESSOR

Two sets of powerful muscles form the walls of your digestive tract. Inner rings of muscle push food along. The pulsing, twisting outer muscles mash the food. Mucous glands, nerves and blood vessels line the whole digestive tract. Mucus aids the food's passage and protects the stomach from its own acids. The glands make enzymes and hormones to break food down. Together, hormones and nerves control digestion.

HANDS ON

Open Wide

❶ Place a small ball inside a stocking. Imagine that the ball is some just-swallowed cheese and the stocking is your digestive tract.

❷ Hold the top of the stocking firmly in one hand. With the other hand, squeeze the stocking just above the ball, moving the ball down. Repeat until the ball reaches the end.

In the same way, the muscular walls of your digestive system contract in waves, moving food along. This is called peristalsis. Next time you take a bite of a sandwich, pay attention to the feeling as the food goes down your throat.

Saliva and teeth transform the sandwich into mush, called a bolus.

Seconds later, a swallow sends the bolus hurtling down the oesophagus, your food tube, to your stomach.

A BUMPY RIDE

Three sets of criss-crossed muscles give your stomach its churning power. Its inner surface is folded and pitted. The folds flatten to make room for food. The tiny gastric pits squirt out enzymes and germ-killing acid. Food doesn't stand a chance.

Your stomach churns. For three hours, it mashes the bolus with digestive juices, turning it into soupy chyme.

Chyme passes into the small intestine, which breaks it into nutrients and wastes. The nutrients seep through the intestine wall.

Blood carries the nutrients to the liver, which turns some into sugar for energy and stores others.

Wastes go into the large intestine, which sucks out the last water and minerals.

As solid waste called faeces, this matter leaves the body through the anus.

NOT SO SMALL

Your small intestine is small only in diameter. This narrow tube is about 5.4 metres (18 ft) long. Thousands of folds and finger-like villi make its surface even larger. Nutrients trickle through the villi into blood vessels. Blood carries the nutrients through your body.

YOU ARE WHAT YOU EAT

The foods you eat help your body in different ways. Fats give you long-term energy. Carbohydrates and sugars provide quick energy. Vitamins and minerals nourish cells and proteins help repair them. Your body needs a balance of these.

ENERGY BANKS

Food energy is measured in kilojoules (calories). If you take in more kilojoules than you use, your body stores the extra as fat. Exercise and balanced eating keep your weight healthy.

Mulberries *Kackstones* *Gravel*

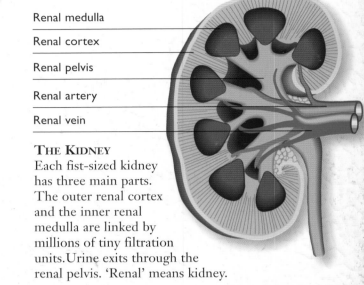

Renal medulla
Renal cortex
Renal pelvis
Renal artery
Renal vein

THE KIDNEY
Each fist-sized kidney has three main parts. The outer renal cortex and the inner renal medulla are linked by millions of tiny filtration units. Urine exits through the renal pelvis. 'Renal' means kidney.

Water Ways

IMAGINE WHAT YOUR house would look like if no one drained the dishwater or took out the rubbish. Ugh! In no time at all, you'd need to move out. Your body must regularly get rid of wastes, too. If it didn't, you would die. Your kidneys and bladder flush out watery wastes. Along with two tubes called the ureters and another called the urethra, they make up your urinary system.

After your cells grab all the nutrients they need from your digested food, they return wastes to your blood. Blood carries these wastes to your kidneys. The kidneys are your body's recycling centre. Each one has a million microscopic filters called nephrons. Each nephron is made up of a knot of tiny blood vessels and a twisted, looped tube. Fluid and wastes pass from the blood vessels into the tube. As they pass through the tube, any water and chemicals needed return to the blood. Extra water, salts and a waste product called urea don't. These become urine. Your kidneys can make more or less urine. In this way, they help keep the chemicals and water in your body balanced.

Urine dribbles from the kidneys into two long, muscled tubes – the ureters. The ureters' walls tighten and relax, pushing urine towards the bladder. The bladder expands. It stores the urine until you decide you've got to go.

DRIP, DRIP
Your kidneys release urine every 10–15 seconds. The urine trickles down two thin tubes, called ureters, into the bladder. You can see this in the coloured X-ray. When half a cup of urine drips down, you feel the urge to go. More than two cups and you'd better find a toilet fast!

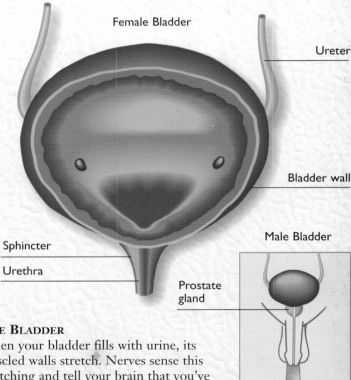

Female Bladder

Ureter

Bladder wall

Male Bladder

Sphincter
Urethra

Prostate gland

THE BLADDER
When your bladder fills with urine, its muscled walls stretch. Nerves sense this stretching and tell your brain that you've got to urinate. The bladder walls tighten. They squeeze the urine out as the sphincter muscles, which usually clamp the bladder shut, open. Urine gushes out of the urethra. The bladders shown here are full. When empty, the bladder is the size of a walnut and shaped like a wine glass.

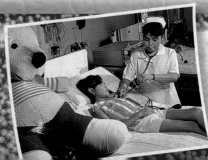

FAILED KIDNEYS
One kidney can do the work of two. But if both fail, poisons build up in the blood. Regular treatments, called dialysis, remove the poisons.

NEW KIDNEYS
A donated kidney can save a life. But not any kidney will do. It must match the receiver's tissue type. Many people die waiting for a matching kidney.

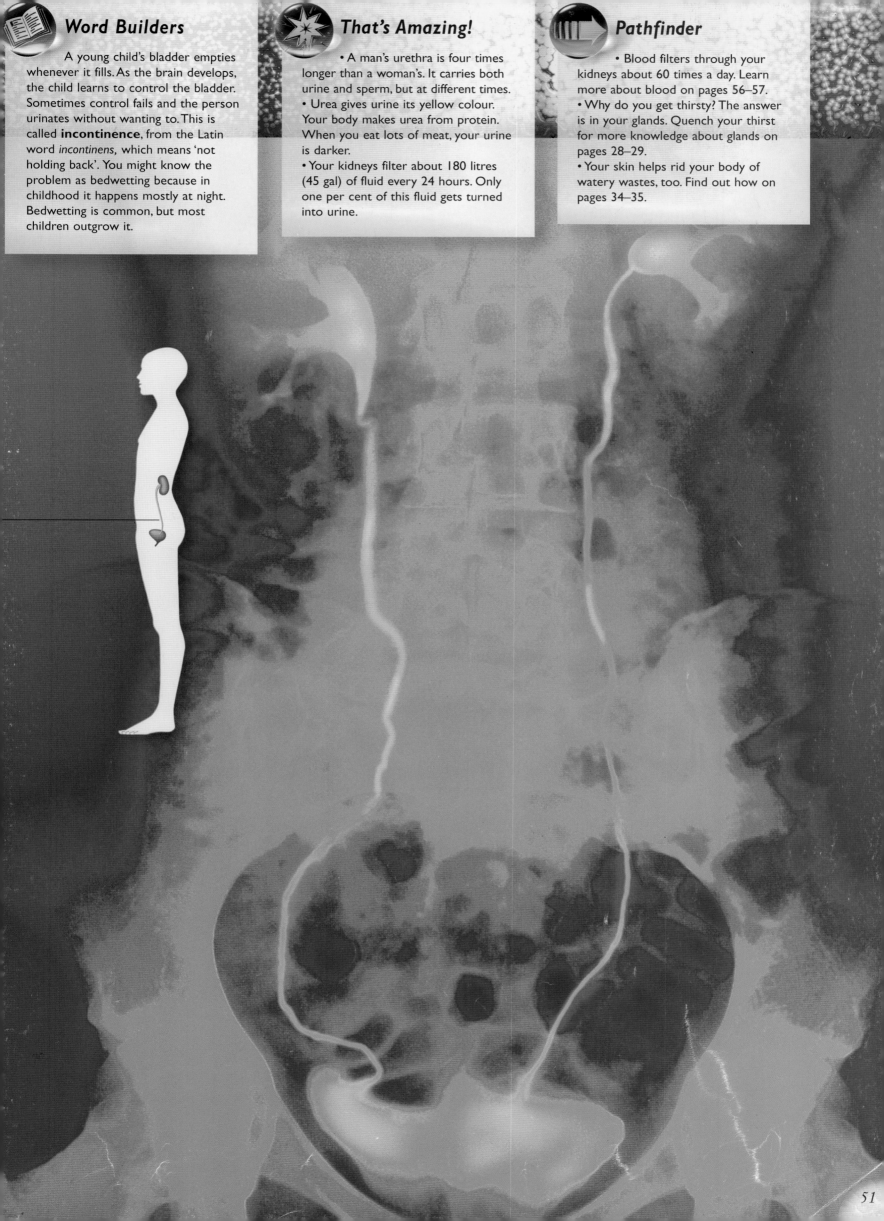

Word Builders

A young child's bladder empties whenever it fills. As the brain develops, the child learns to control the bladder. Sometimes control fails and the person urinates without wanting to. This is called **incontinence**, from the Latin word *incontinens*, which means 'not holding back'. You might know the problem as bedwetting because in childhood it happens mostly at night. Bedwetting is common, but most children outgrow it.

That's Amazing!

• A man's urethra is four times longer than a woman's. It carries both urine and sperm, but at different times.
• Urea gives urine its yellow colour. Your body makes urea from protein. When you eat lots of meat, your urine is darker.
• Your kidneys filter about 180 litres (45 gal) of fluid every 24 hours. Only one per cent of this fluid gets turned into urine.

Pathfinder

• Blood filters through your kidneys about 60 times a day. Learn more about blood on pages 56–57.
• Why do you get thirsty? The answer is in your glands. Quench your thirst for more knowledge about glands on pages 28–29.
• Your skin helps rid your body of watery wastes, too. Find out how on pages 34–35.

Take a Breath

HOW LONG CAN you hold your breath? Probably not more than a minute or two. Your brain won't let you. It and every other part of you need a never-ending flow of oxygen. That oxygen arrives with every breath you take. Your cells use oxygen for energy. If you try to cut off your body's oxygen supply, your brain takes over. It forces you to breathe so that your cells – and you – won't die.

Breathing does more than bring oxygen to your body. It also removes waste gases, such as carbon dioxide. Your lungs, heart and blood work together to swap the good gas for the bad. Here's how:

Thousands of tiny air tubes called bronchioles make up your spongy lungs. Each bronchiole ends in a cluster of even tinier air sacs, called alveoli. A net of blood vessels covers the alveoli. The walls of the blood vessels and alveoli are so thin that gases pass easily from one to the other. Oxygen seeps from the alveoli into the blood to begin its journey to your cells. Blood returning to the lungs carries the gases the body doesn't need. Breathe out. The harmful gases are gone. Breathe in. A fresh load of life-giving oxygen is on its way. Each day, you breathe in some 18,900 litres (5,000 gal) of air.

Bronchi

Thousands of bronchioles branch through each lung. They lead to 600–700 million alveoli.

HANDS ON

Work It Out

When you exercise, your lungs get a workout, too. Your hardworking muscles need more oxygen, so you breathe more rapidly. Your heart beats faster to speed the oxygen to your arms and legs. You can test this for yourself.

1 Set a stopwatch for two minutes. Count the number of times you breathe per minute while at rest. In and out again counts as one breath.

2 Now jog in place for two minutes. Count your breaths again. How long does your breathing take to return to normal after exercise?

Muscle   Bronchiole

BREATHE DEEPLY
Whoosh! Air rushes into your nose and down your windpipe. It flows into your bronchi, the two main passages into your lungs. It charges down smaller bronchi and into even smaller tubes called bronchioles, finally landing in the alveoli. Whoosh! Air rushes out. At rest, you breathe in and out about 15 times a minute.

PRIME MOVERS
Your lungs sit in the muscled chamber of your chest. A membrane called the pleura attaches them to the ribs in front. The lungs rest on the diaphragm, your main breathing muscle. When you breathe in, muscles pull your ribs up and out. Your diaphragm flattens. Your lungs expand and suck in air. When you breathe out, the rib cage sinks and the diaphragm springs up, squeezing the air out of your lungs.

Breastbo

Lung

Diaphragm
flattens

Diaphragm
springs up

Ribs

Word Builders

The lung disease **pneumonia** gets its name from the ancient Greek word for 'air', *pneuma*. Some early thinkers believed that pneuma was the spirit, the force that made them move and gave them life. Others thought it fanned a fire in the heart and so kept them alive. They knew that this pneuma flowed into the *pneumon*, the lung.

That's Amazing!

• Pure oxygen is dangerous for you. It can damage your lungs. Air is only 20 per cent oxygen.
• You breathe more rapidly when you're sick. Your body needs more energy to help you heal, so it uses more oxygen.
• One unfortunate man hiccupped 20 to 25 times a minute for 68 years. He still led a normal life. He married twice and had eight children.

Pathfinder

• Half your heart supplies blood only to your lungs. Learn more on pages 54–55.
• Your nose takes good care of your lungs. It warms the air you breathe and filters out dust and germs. Go to pages 24–25.
• Both food and air travel down your throat. Find out how they get to the right places on pages 26–27.

Cartilage

Blood vessels

Alveoli

INSIDE STORY

Troubled Breath

The air we breathe isn't pure. It carries dust and dirt, pollen and pollutants. In some people, these substances irritate the lungs. Air passages swell. Muscles tighten. The person wheezes, struggling for breath. This condition is called asthma. It's the most common cause of chronic illness in children. Inhaled medicine helps control asthma. Better yet, many children outgrow the disease. No one outgrows the lung damage that smoking can cause, however. Tobacco smoke is poison to the lungs. It is the major cause of lung cancer.

INSIDE AN ALVEOLI
Each tiny alveoli balloons out as it fills with air. Oxygen seeps out through its walls and into tiny blood vessels. Carbon dioxide seeps in and is exhaled.

THIN AIR
Your brain controls how fast you breathe. It monitors signals from your muscles and the amount of carbon dioxide in your blood. Too much carbon dioxide and you breathe harder, sucking in more oxygen for your cells. You breathe hard at high altitudes because there is less air, and you get less oxygen with each breath.

Windpipe (trachea)

Right lung

Left lung

THE BIG PICTURE
Your right lung has three sections, or lobes. Your left has two. It's smaller to make room for your heart.

Bronchi leading to bronchioles and alveoli

Diaphragm

Your pulse tells you how fast your heart is beating.

Heart of the Matter

PLACE YOUR FINGERS on your wrist. The beat you feel is the steady pumping of your blood. Each day, your blood circles your body over and over. It delivers food and oxygen to your cells and removes wastes. It carries hormones to their targets and helps you fight disease. It travels through a vast network of tubes called blood vessels, pumped by your powerful heart.

Your heart is slightly bigger than your fist. Its unique cardiac muscle never tires and never rests. It keeps blood streaming steadily through your body.

When your body needs more energy, your heart responds. Jog for a short time and you'll feel it pounding. The harder pumping speeds blood along. Oxygen-rich blood flows from your heart into arteries. It delivers the oxygen, as well as food, to hungry cells. It picks up carbon dioxide and other wastes, then flows back to the heart through veins. Along the way, your kidneys and liver filter the blood. The returning blood surges into your heart. A powerful contraction sends it to the lungs, where the blood dumps carbon dioxide and picks up oxygen. It flows back into the heart, then hits the road again.

INSIDE STORY
Heart Stopper

The place is Provident Hospital, Chicago, U.S.A. A man has been stabbed in the heart. Dr. Daniel Hale Williams opens the man's chest and closes the wound. The man lives. Sounds like everyday emergency room surgery? Think again. The year was 1893, and Dr. Williams had just performed the world's first successful heart operation. Today doctors can not only repair the heart – they can even replace it.

THROUGH THICK AND THIN
Capillaries are the body's smallest blood vessels. Their walls are only a single cell thick. Nutrients pass easily through these walls into the cells of your tissues. Arteries and veins are much thicker and tougher. Their walls have three layers: an outer coat, muscle and a lining. Thin membranes separate these layers.

Blood cell **Capillary**

THE HEART'S HELPERS
Arteries carry blood away from the heart. Their thick, elastic muscles help push the blood along. They also make a gas – nitric oxide – that relaxes their muscles. When the artery muscles relax, blood flows more easily.

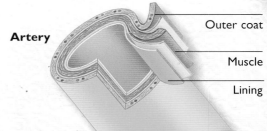

Artery

Outer coat

Muscle

Lining

FORWARD HO!
Veins carry blood back to the heart. Those in arms and legs have valves to keep blood from flowing backwards.

Vein

Valve

Outer coat

Muscle

Lining

HANDS ON
Bailing Water

Your heart pumps about one-fifth of a litre (one-third of a pint) of blood into your arteries with every beat. It does this 60 to 80 times a minute. Try it yourself:

❶ Get two buckets and a cup. Fill one bucket with water.

❷ Try bailing a cup of water from one bucket to the other, 70 times a minute.

LISTENING IN
Doctors use a stethoscope to listen to your heart. Unusual sounds can tell the doctor that the heart valves are not opening or shutting properly. If the valves are not doing their job, the heart can't pump efficiently.

Word Builders

Your arteries throb with every beat of your heart. This is the **pulse** you feel at your wrist. The word pulse comes from the Latin *pulsus*, which means 'beating'. A piece of special heart tissue called a pacemaker sets and controls the beat. **Pace** comes from the Latin word *passus*, which means 'step'.

That's Amazing!

• Most of your capillaries are so thin that red blood cells must line up in single file to get through.
• Growing takes work, so a child's heart beats faster than an adult's to supply extra energy. A child's heart rate is about 90 beats a minute. An adult's is 70. An infant's heart beats about 120 times a minute.

Pathfinder

• Your heart beats almost 40 million times a year. Each beat pushes about five tablespoons (70 ml) of blood into your arteries. Learn more about blood on pages 56–57.
• Your body has a second transportation system. Find out more on pages 58–59.
• Your brain cells begin to die after just a few minutes without blood. Go to pages 16–17 to learn about your brain.

TWO PUMPS IN ONE

The four chambers of your heart form two pumps. The right side pumps blood from the body to the lungs. The left side pumps oxygen-rich blood from the lungs to the body.

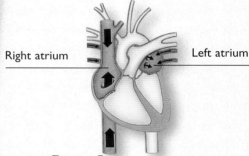

Right atrium — Left atrium

BLOOD IN

The top chambers of the heart, the atria, relax. De-oxygenated blood from the body pours into the right atrium. Oxygen-rich blood from the lungs fills the left.

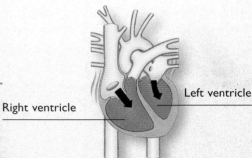

Right ventricle — Left ventricle

VALVES OPEN

The atria contract. Blood pushes open the valves leading to the heart's pumping chambers. These chambers, the ventricles, fill with blood.

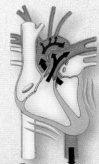

BLOOD OUT

The ventricles contract, forcing open the valves to the arteries. Blood shoots into the arteries. As the valves close, they make the familiar sounds of a heartbeat: *boom boom*.

Major vein

Major artery

Heart

PASSING THROUGH

Your blood vessels are your body's road system. The major veins and arteries are the wide motorways. They exit into smaller veins and arteries that supply each part of the body with its own local roads. Tiny capillaries are the country lanes. They connect veins and arteries and reach every tissue cell.

GO WITH THE FLOW
What's in your blood? What does blood do for you? What happens to the blood as it streams through your body? Find out below. Start with 'Busy Blood', and then go with the flow.

It's in the Blood

LIKE A DROP of pond water, your blood teems with life. Billions of blood cells cruise your body, travelling in a sea of straw-coloured plasma. Plasma makes up most of your blood. It brings nourishment to your cells and carries wastes away.

Plasma's main passengers are red blood cells. These are your body's delivery people. They call on other cells, dropping off oxygen and picking up carbon dioxide. Red blood cells look like tyres with dents instead of holes.

White blood cells prowl through your bloodstream too. They protect you against foreign invaders. Some travel to specific tissues and stand guard. Others keep sailing until you're injured or sick. Then they surge into your tissues to battle with germs.

Platelets, another component of plasma, aren't whole cells at all. They're fragments of certain white blood cells. When you bleed, they trigger clotting. This vital service helps you heal. It keeps your blood inside your vessels, streaming through your body on its life-preserving rounds.

INSIDE STORY
The Blood That Binds

The surgeon's tools lie on the tray. There are scalpels, tweezers and glue. Glue? That's right. Surgical glue uses the same clotting chemicals as your body. These are fibrinogen and thrombin. When you bleed, they latch together to make fibrin. Threads of fibrin form the mesh on which blood clots. The glue makes fibrin, too. Surgeons use it to stop the flow of blood from small, hard-to-seal vessels and for skin grafts. They don't have to remove the glue. The body absorbs it.

BUSY BLOOD
Blood carries hundreds of vital substances around your body. That's why blood tests reveal so much about your health.

WHY IS YOUR BLOOD RED?
Red blood cells give blood its colour. A protein in the cells called haemoglobin latches on to oxygen. When it does, it turns bright red.

BLOOD CARRIES:
• sugar, proteins and salts
• vitamins and minerals
• wastes
• hormones
• germ-fighting chemicals
• oxygen and carbon dioxide

THIN BLOOD
Anaemia is a blood condition. Someone with anaemia can't make enough red blood cells.

THE PUMP
Your heart keeps your blood moving through your body.

NEED RED CELLS?
As your kidneys clean your blood, they track oxygen levels. If levels fall too low, they tell bone marrow to make more red cells.

THE SUPPLIERS
Red blood cells ferry oxygen to every cell in your tissues. They carry away waste gases. You have 700 red cells for every white one.

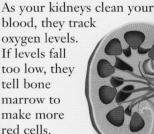

Word Builders

If you ever need blood, your doctor will check your **blood group** before giving it to you. Your blood group tells which chemical markers your red blood cells carry. The markers are A and B. They are named because of the order in which they were discovered. Your blood group can be A, B, AB (if you have both) or O (if you have neither).

That's Amazing!

• All the platelets in your body wouldn't fill two teaspoons. Yet you have millions of them.
• Dead red blood cells give faeces most of its colour.
• White blood cells aren't really white. They're clear.
• You have about 96,000 kilometres (60,000 mi) of blood vessels.

Pathfinder

• Your bones make your blood cells. What else does bone do? Go to pages 40–41.
• Each red blood cell makes its rounds 300,000 times before it dies. Learn more about cells on pages 10–11.
• Your white blood cells attack invading germs. Find out how they protect you on pages 58–59.

WHEN IS YOUR BLOOD BLUE?
When haemoglobin drops off oxygen, it loses its bright red colour. The blood looks blue. You can see it in your veins.

A CLOT FORMS
Platelets release chemicals that make fibrin. The thread-like fibrin traps platelets and red blood cells (right). A clot forms, which stops the bleeding.

HOW MUCH BLOOD DO YOU NEED?

◯ 1.7 litres (3 pt)
◯ 11.4 litres (20 pt)
✓ 4.5 litres (8 pt)

That's how much is moving through your body right now.

Your Blood. Plasma makes up 55 per cent of your blood. It's mostly water.

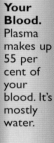

Red blood cells make up 45 per cent of your blood.

ORGAN DUTY
The liver cleans the blood. It also grabs nutrients for processing, then returns them to the bloodstream.

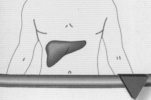

Splinter

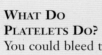

BLOOD TO THE RESCUE
Ouch! Injured cells signal for help. Platelets stick together to plug the wound.

A TOUGH SCAB
The fibrin, trapped cells and fluid from the blood harden into a protective scab. Healing begins.

BLOOD TYPES
The blood you get from a donor has to be compatible with your own. If not, your body will reject it. Your blood group tells which types of blood you can receive.

SPLEEN CLEANING
Your spleen removes dead red blood cells from circulation. It also makes some white cells.

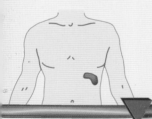

WHAT DO PLATELETS DO?
You could bleed to death without platelets. They bunch up at the site of an injury anywhere in your body. They plug the wound to stop the bleeding.

GERM PATROL
White blood cells under a scab gobble up germs. They ward off infection.

LIFESAVING BANKS
Blood banks test and store donated blood.

R. I. P.
Most blood cells have a short life. A red cell lives about 120 days. Some white cells live only about a week. They die protecting you.

THE DEFENDERS
White blood cells are the body's protectors. They seek, round up and destroy foreign invaders. They mop up after a battle with viruses, bacteria or other aliens.

REPLACEMENT BLOOD
Lost blood is replaced quickly. Bone marrow churns out millions of red blood cells a second.

EMERGENCY!
This time you're badly injured. You're in surgery. You're losing more blood than your body can replace. You need new blood fast. Donated blood can help you.

White blood cells and platelets make up less than one per cent of your blood.

Germs can gather in a hair follicle, causing an infection. This tender lump is called a boil.

Protecting Us

OUCH! A BEE STING. You feel pain. Blood rushes into your finger. The finger reddens and swells. Your immune system is on the attack.

Your immune system protects you from poisons and germs. It helps heal injuries. It is made up of white blood cells, the chemicals they make and the organs that produce them. Some white blood cells live in your tissues. They attack any harmful substance that comes near. Others patrol your body. They charge to an injury. They seek and destroy invaders like bacteria and viruses.

Any invader or injury can trigger your immune system's general alarm. Red, hot, swollen tissue is the result. Your body targets specific invaders, too. Invader cells display a unique chemical ID called an antigen. These IDs let your immune system tell the good guys – your cells – from the bad. Special immune cells recognize every possible antigen. Called B and T cells, each one prowls through the body, searching for a specific invader. If it finds its suspect, the cell reproduces rapidly. It creates an army to fight this one enemy. T cells kill directly. B cells mark the enemy with chemicals called antibodies, then other cells destroy it. The first time a foreign agent invades, you don't have many antibodies for it. You may become ill, but the next time, invaders beware. That's why you don't get diseases such as chicken pox twice.

ARMED AND READY

An army of specialists is ready to protect you. These specialists are different types of white blood cell (they are coloured cream in the picture so that you can see them). Each protects you in its own way. Neutrophils swoop in and destroy germs at the site of injury. Lymphocytes, which include B and T cells, hunt down specific invaders. Huge macrophages swallow germs. They also suck up the rubbish left by an immune system attack.

Macrophages respond to the immune system's general alarm. The largest white blood cells, they gobble up invaders. This type of attack is called phagocytosis.

• Skin, mucus and saliva are your body's front-line defences. They keep germs from getting in.
• T cells mature in your thymus, but the thymus shrinks as you age. In children, it's the size of a lemon. In adults, it's the size of an acorn.
• The brain and immune system 'talk' to each other. Your emotions and stress level can influence how well your immune system works.

• You can inherit allergies. Go to pages 12–13 to learn more.
• The lymphatic system not only fights disease, it also helps maintain the body's fluid balance. To find out why this is important, go to pages 50–51.
• Your useful lymph aids digestion, too. It carries fats out of the digestive tract. Learn about digestion on pages 48–49.
• Is there vegetable vaccine in your future? Find out on pages 60–61.

This **T cell** spies its suspect. It multiplies, forming an army of thousands. The army attacks. It makes chemicals that directly destroy its target.

Neutrophils attack any foreigner in sight. This one is lunching on a long bacterium.

B cells don't attack directly. They release antibodies into the area. This allows macrophages to recognize the invaders and gobble them up.

THE GERM FIGHTER

If you've had swollen glands, you've felt one of your body's top germ fighters. The glands are lymph nodes. A milky fluid called lymph flows around the body through its own system of vessels and nodes. This is called the lymphatic system. Packed with white blood cells, these nodes filter germs and debris. Your lymphatic system protects in other ways, too. T cells mature in the thymus. The spleen makes immune cells and filters blood. The lymph fluid itself carries foreign agents away from tissues. Cleansed lymph pours into the bloodstream through lymph ducts, carrying white blood cells with it.

Thymus

Lymph node

Spleen

Lymph vessel

DOWN TIME

Your immune system can sometimes let you down. It can over-react to pollen (below), dust or even chocolate. The result? Allergies.

LOSING BATTLE

Your immune system can lose battles, too. When it does, you become ill. Some diseases attack immune cells themselves, and destroy the body's ability to defend itself. AIDS is one such disease.

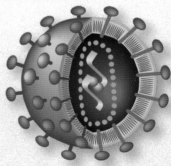

MISTAKEN IDENTITY

Sometimes the immune system mistakes the body's own cells for aliens. It attacks. The body destroys its own tissues. This happens to the joints in rheumatoid arthritis. The disease causes joints to swell and fill with fluid. They become stiff and painful to move.

GENE-IES
Your genes may grant your future health wishes. One day, doctors will test your genes to choose the best medicine for you. They will replace faulty or missing genes that play a role in diseases such as cancer.

COPY SHEEP
Cloned sheep may provide factories for human drugs. Genes are changed so that the sheep make these drug products in their milk.

Future Us

WHAT CAN A MUMMY tell us about the body of the future? More than you might think. Thanks to modern imaging, scientists have looked beneath a mummy's wrapping. There lay the remains of a body much like ours. It showed signs of our diseases, too. Ancient Egyptians felt the pain of arthritis and tooth decay. They died of heart attacks and strokes.

The human body has changed little in the past 5,000 years. It is not likely to change much in the next few thousand either. Humans will still walk upright. They will run five fingers through their hair. They will sleep and dream and fall in love, but they will live longer, healthier lives. As scientists unravel more of the body's mysteries, our ability to improve health grows. New vaccines may prevent killer diseases such as cancer or AIDS. Foods from cereals to chewing gum may be treated to help boost health and fight disease. A life span of 120 years won't be uncommon, and some scientists think we can extend even that.

No matter how long humans live, their lives won't be illness-free. New viruses will outwit their immune systems. The tools they'll have to fight them are as unknown to us now as vaccines and imaging machines were to our ancestors. Human bodies may stay the same, but people will learn more about themselves and protect themselves differently in the future.

FUTURE HEALING

Might plastic muscles replace damaged ones? Could nerve cells added to the brain repair damage from stroke or brain diseases? Could a person's own cells be grown in the laboratory then used to rebuild damaged tissues? Perhaps. Research in all these areas is underway. In fact, doctors can already grow cartilage-making cells in the laboratory. These cells are then put back into the body, where they make new cartilage.

INSIDE STORY

Remote Surgery

The surgeon prepares to operate. She slips her hands into her gloves. These gloves aren't thin and sterile. They are threaded with wires that transmit pressure. The surgeon sits down at the computer. Her gloved hands grasp two joysticks. She is ready to begin. Her patient is ready, too. He lies in an operating room thousands of miles away. Robot arms hover above his kidney. As the surgeon guides the joysticks, the robot operates. Science fiction? No. Surgeons have already carried out remote surgery. One day, it will be routine.

Robots are aiding surgeons in another way, too. Robot fingers can fit through openings too small for human hands. They will be used to do more and more complex surgery.

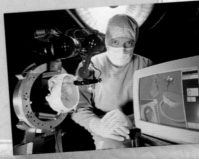

SUPER SCIENCE
A horse-riding accident put Christopher Reeve, Hollywood's Superman, in a wheelchair. His spinal cord was damaged, paralysing him from his neck down. Will he walk again? Perhaps. Scientists are looking for ways to heal damaged nerves and to make new ones grow. They are designing tiny computers to do the work of nerves and so move muscles. Super science may yet help Superman.

Word Builders

A **clone** is an exact copy of an individual. It is grown from a single cell of the original. Scientists have cloned adult sheep and cows. Might scientists someday clone humans? If they could, the clone and the original would never be exactly the same. Each person's life is unique. Every experience shapes both mind and body.

That's Amazing!

• People today are about 8 centimetres (3 in) taller than 200 years ago because of better nutrition.
• Our cells have built-in time clocks. They reproduce a set number of times, then die. In laboratories, scientists have reset these clocks, keeping cells alive longer. Someday they may be able to do this in the body to slow ageing.

Pathfinder

• New contact lenses could give us better than 20/20 vision. To gain insight into eyes, turn to pages 20–21.
• Gene therapy may make bald heads and grey hair a thing of the past. Why do people lose their hair and turn grey? The answer is on pages 36–37.

BYE-BYE, NEEDLES
Some day, vegetables might replace injections. Scientists are working on special 'veggie vaccines'. Instead of getting a flu injection, you'll get a dose of the vaccine in your food. Diabetics may be able to say goodbye to needles, too. Insulin inhalers are on the way.

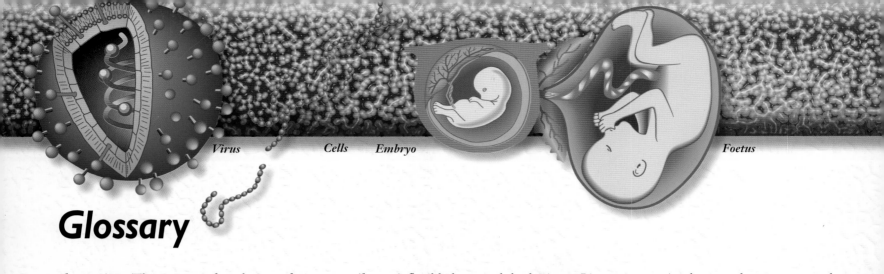

Virus *Cells* *Embryo* *Foetus*

Glossary

absorption The passage of a substance from one part of the body to another through a thin barrier, such as the passage of digested food into the bloodstream through the wall of the small intestine.

alveoli Tiny air pockets in the lungs that are covered with a net of blood vessels. Gases pass between the alveoli and blood vessels.

antibody A protein produced by special blood cells to help fight and destroy germs.

artery A muscular blood vessel that carries fresh (oxygenated) blood away from the heart.

atria The two chambers of the heart that collect blood as it comes in.

axon The long arm of a neuron that passes messages to the next cell. The messages travel down the axon as electric pulses.

bacteria One-cell beings. Some bacteria are germs that make people sick.

blood–brain barrier One of the brain's protections. It controls which substances enter the brain from the blood.

blood cells The two kinds of cell that make up some of your blood. Red blood cells deliver oxygen to other cells and pick up carbon dioxide. White blood cells fight off foreign invaders.

bolus A lump of chewed food that enters the throat when swallowing.

capillary The smallest kind of blood vessel. Capillaries reach every tissue cell in the body.

carbon dioxide A gas that is a normal waste produced by cells when they use energy. It is transported in the bloodstream to the lungs, then it is breathed out.

cardiac Anything to do with the heart.

cartilage A flexible but tough body tissue. It forms part of the framework of the body and covers the ends of some bones.

cell The smallest unit of life that is able to function independently. The human body is an organized mass of cells.

cerebral Anything to do with the brain.

chromosomes Structures containing DNA and proteins that carry genetic instructions. Humans have 46 chromosomes. They are stored in a cell's nucleus.

chyme Soupy lumps of partly digested food that move from the stomach into the small intestine.

cilia Fine, hair-like parts of cells that sway back and forth.

cochlea The part of the inner ear in which sound waves are turned into nerve signals.

cone A type of cell in the eye's retina that picks up colours and fine details, then sends this information as nerve signals to the brain.

cortex The outer layer of a body part such as a kidney or the brain.

dermis The inner layer of skin that contains blood vessels, nerves, sweat glands and hair roots.

DNA The molecule that contains genes. It looks like a twisted ladder. DNA stands for deoxyribonucleic acid.

embryo An unborn organism in the earliest stages of development. In humans, this is from about one week to eight weeks inside the womb.

enamel The hard outer coating of teeth.

endocrine system A network of glands that produce hormones.

enzyme A substance that acts on another to change it. Food is broken down with the help of enzymes.

epidermis The outer layer of skin. It is made of new skin cells at the base and tough, dead skin cells on the surface.

fertilization The union of female and male sex cells.

foetus An unborn individual during the later stages of development. In humans, this is from the ninth week of pregnancy through to birth.

follicle A tiny opening, such as the one from which a hair grows.

gamete A sperm or egg; a sex cell.

genes The blueprints for life that individuals inherit from their parents. Genes are carried on chromosomes.

gestation The time a baby spends developing inside its mother's womb.

glands Parts of the body that produce hormones, sweat, saliva, and other substances.

gustatory Anything to do with the sense of taste.

hormones The body's chemical messengers. They help control many body functions according to the body's needs.

immune Able to fight and destroy bacteria, viruses or other germs so that they cannot harm the body.

implant To place in the body. For instance, an artificial pacemaker may be implanted.

inflammation A reaction of the body to a harmful substance or injury. This reaction usually involves swelling, pain and warmth.

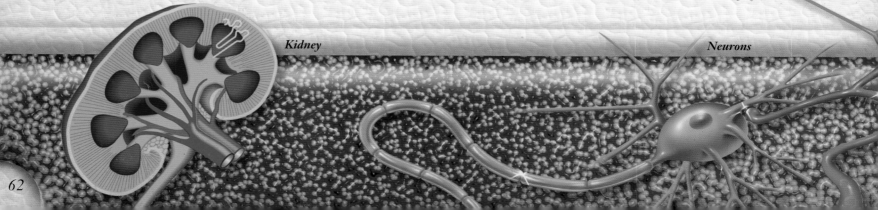

Kidney *Neurons*

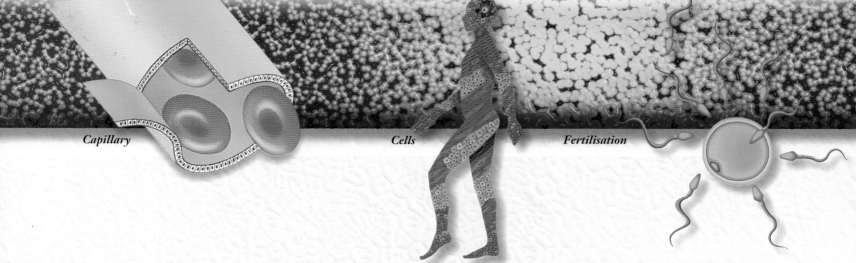

Capillary *Cells* *Fertilisation*

keratin A protein that toughens skin, nails and hair.

ligament A flexible band of tissue that attaches one bone to another at the joint. Ligaments also attach teeth to the jaw.

lymph A pale fluid that is made primarily of white blood cells. It is important in fighting infection. Lymph travels through the body in special vessels and pours into the bloodstream through lymph ducts.

lymph nodes Small organs that filter lymph and store white blood cells.

lymphocyte A type of white blood cell.

medulla The innermost part of an organ such as a kidney.

melanin The body's main natural colouring substance or pigment, which gives skin, eyes and hair their colour. The greater the amount of melanin, the darker the skin's colour.

membrane A thin protective barrier around cells or organs, such as the cell membrane around a cell or the mucous membrane lining the nose, mouth, airways and digestive tract.

meninges The membranes that cover and protect the brain and spinal cord.

menstruation The breakdown and loss of the lining of the womb that happens every month if a woman's egg has not been fertilized.

mucus A thick, slimy substance that moistens and protects some body parts, such as the lining of the nose.

myelin A material that insulates the axons of many nerve cells.

myofibrils Fibres inside muscle cells.

nerves Bundles of long, thin neurons that connect the brain to the rest of the body.

neuron A nerve cell.

neurotransmitter A chemical that ferries messages across the gap between neurons.

nutrient A substance that the body can use for energy, growth or repair.

olfactory Anything to do with the sense of smell.

organ A collection of tissues that has a specific function. The brain, heart, stomach and kidneys are organs.

organelle The parts of a cell. Each has a different job.

oxygen A gas that is breathed in and transported to every cell in the body through the bloodstream. Oxygen helps the cells release energy from food.

pacemaker A piece of specialized, electrically charged muscle that controls the heart's rhythm.

placenta The blood-rich organ that lines the mother's womb to provide nourishment for a developing foetus. The placenta comes out after the baby is born.

plasma The pale, watery fluid that makes up most of your blood. It brings nourishment, hormones and germ-fighting substances to your cells. It carries away wastes.

proteins The chemicals that are the building blocks of cells.

renal Anything to do with the kidneys.

rod A type of cell in the retina of the eye that can pick up shapes in dim light. Rod cells cannot detect colours and fine details.

saliva A fluid made by glands in the mouth and throat to begin the process of digestion.

scan A computerized picture of the inside of the body created by a special machine.

synapse The gap between each nerve cell.

system A collection of organs that work together to carry out a job in the body. An example is the digestive system.

tendon A tough rope of tissue that attaches a muscle to a bone.

tissue Cells joined with others like themselves to carry out a specific function.

transplant To replace a damaged body part with a functioning one from a donor.

urea The chemical waste that gives urine its colour.

ureter One of the two tubes that carry urine from the kidneys to the bladder.

urethra The tube that carries urine out of the body.

valve A flap in a blood vessel that opens only one way so that blood cannot flow backwards.

vein A vessel that usually carries used (de-oxygenated) blood back to the heart.

ventricles The two chambers of the heart that pump blood to the body (the left ventricle) and to the lungs (the right ventricle).

villi Tiny, finger-shaped projections from the lining of the small intestine.

virus A very simple micro-organism that must invade living cells to grow and multiply. Viruses cause disease.

zygote A just-fertilized egg.

Ureter *Rods and Cones*

Index

The publishers would like to thank the following for their assistance in the preparation of this book: Mallory Baker, Barbara Bakowski, Herman Beckelman, Robert Beckelman, James Clark, Robert Goodell Jr., Steve Ottinoski, Jason Prentice, Lloyd Prentice, Dina Rubin, Jennifer Themel, Stephen Vincent, Michael Wolfman, D.D.S, Vinnie Zara..
Our special thanks to the following children who feature in the photographs: Michelle Burk, Simon Burk, Elliot Burton, Clay Canda-Cameron, Lisa Chan, Anton Crowden and Henry (the dog), Amanda Hanani, Mark Humphries, Gina Lamprell, Louis Lamprell, Bianca Laurence, Kyle Linnahan, Daniel Price, Rebecca Price, Poppy Rourke, Zoe Rourke, Jeremy Sequeira, Julian Sequeira, Gemma Smith, Gerard Smith, Chrisopher Stirling, Lucy Vaux, Craig Wilford, Amanda Wilson.
PICTURE CREDITS (t=top, b=bottom, l=left, r=right, c=center, e=extreme, f=flap, F=Front, C=Cover, B=Back). (TPL=The Photo Library, Sydney, SPL=Science Photo Library.) AdLibitum 5b, 6br, 7c, 7bl, 8bl, 12bl, 15r, 15b, 16l, 20/21b, 20tl, 20cl, 20bl, 21tr, 21b, 22tr, 22br, 23tl, 24c, 24br, 26l, 26cr, 26b, 27bl, 27br, 28bl, 28br, 29br, 30bl, 31bl, 31tr, 32tr, 32bl, 33tl, 34c, 34tr, 34br, 35bl, 36/37c, 36tr, 36br, 38tr, 38cl, 38bl, 39c, 40tr, 40cr, 42c, 47br, 48br, 49tr, 52c, 54tl, 54cl, 54bl, 61br (M. Kaniewski).
AP/AAP 19br, 60tr, 60bl. Auscape 37bl (Chassenet-BSIP), 37br (Estiot-BSIP), 25tr (Laurent-Bouhier-BSIP). Baxter Immuno Aktiengesellschaft 56bl. E. T. Archive 58tr. The Granger Collection 48bl. The Image Bank 54crt, 60bc (Flip Chalfant), 31cr (J. P. Kelly), 57cr (J. Stuart). McLean Hospital 17cr. Private photograph usage by permission of M. Rourke 36tc. TPL 28cr (E. Anderson), 37cl (D. Bosler) 11b (D. Becker) 19tr (SPL/D. Besford), 59tl (SPL/Dr A. Brody), 8br (SPL/ Dr J. Burgess) 28bl (M. Clarke)49br (D. Day) 53bl (M. Delmasso) 19bl (Hulton-Deutsch), 37cl (Lori Adamski Peek), 14b (Z. Kaluzny), 55l (V. Michaels), 31t (NIH/Science Source), 33bl, 44tr (S. Peters), 8tr, 35tr, 40cb, 41cl, 49l, 57cb (SPL), 50bl (SPL/O. Burriel), 22/23c (SPL/Prof. P. Cull), 34tl (SPL/M. Dohrn), 45cr, 47cl, 57t (SPL/Eye of Science), 60c (SPL/K. Gulbrandsen), 49cr (SPL/M. Kage), 35tl, 45c, 59br (SPL/Dr P. Marazzi), 40cl, 46br 53cr, 57b (SPL/Prof. P Motta), 24bl (SPL/Motta/Anatomy/Sapienza), 18b (SPL/A. Pasieka), 51c (SPL/Salisbury Hospital), 24tr (SPL/A. Syred), 60tl (SPL/G. Tompkinson), 13br (SPL/H. Young), 10bl (D. Struthers) 13tr (U.B.H Trust), 29bl (USDA/Science Source), 44tl (C. Thatcher). Rainbow 50br (H. Morgan). University of Chicago 54tr. Warren Museum/Harvard Medical School 18c.
ILLUSTRATION CREDITS
Susanna Addario 7tl, 9br, 16/17c, 16t, 16bl, 16br, 17tr, 17bl, 18/19c, 18t, 18cl, 19cr. Martin Camm 12tl. Amy and Sam Collins/Art and Science Inc. 33tr, 40t, 40br, 40/41c, 41b, 46crt, 46bl, 52/53c, 52t, 52b, 53br. Marcus Cremonese 4tr, 6cr, 6r, 7br, 10/11c, 10t, 11tr, 11cr, 11br, 12/13c, 12b, 13b, 28r, 46crb, 47cr, 47bl, 50t, 50l, 50cr, 50br, 51l, 56/57c, 57r, 58/59c, 58t, 59cr, 59bc, 62t, 62bl, 63tr, 63tc, 63bl. Dr. Levent Efe 55b. Christer Eriksson 7tr, 8tl, 8tr, 20/21c, 20bl, 20br, 21r, 21bl, 21br, 29c, 63br. Peg Gerrity 7cr, 26t, 26c, 26r, 27c, 46tr, 48t, 48/49c, 49bl. Gino Hasler 4br, 14bl, 14c, 22br, 23b, 24tc, 24tr, 25l, 25cr, 25br, 32cr, 32br, 36l, 37tr, 38/39b, 38tl, 38tr, 38cr, 47tr, 54r, 55r, 56c. Karen Hinton (Cochlear Limited, Australia) 23tr. Frank Knight 7cl, 24tl. Jeff Lang 22t. Stuart McVicar (Digital Manipulation) 8/9c, 60/61c. Siri Mills 6cr, 14/15c, 15bl, 62br. Spencer Phippen 33br, 44/45c. Claudia Saraceni 12tc, 30/31bl. Peter Schouten 12tr. Marco Sparciari 4cr. Kate Sweeney 5tr, 33cl, 42/43c, 42/43b, 42t, 42br, 43b. Thomas Trojer 30/31c. Rod Westblade 34/35b.
COVER CREDITS Susanna Addario FCtl. AdLibitum FCc (M.Kaniewski) Sam & Amy Collins/Art and Science Inc. FCcr, Ffb. Marcus Cremonese FCtr, FCcl, FCbc, BCcr. Christer Eriksson BCbr, Bfb. Peg Gerrity Fft. Gino Hasler FCbr, Bft, BCbl, BCt. Siri Mills FCbl, BCbc. Claudia Saraceni/Thomas Trojer FCg. Rod Westblade Bfc.

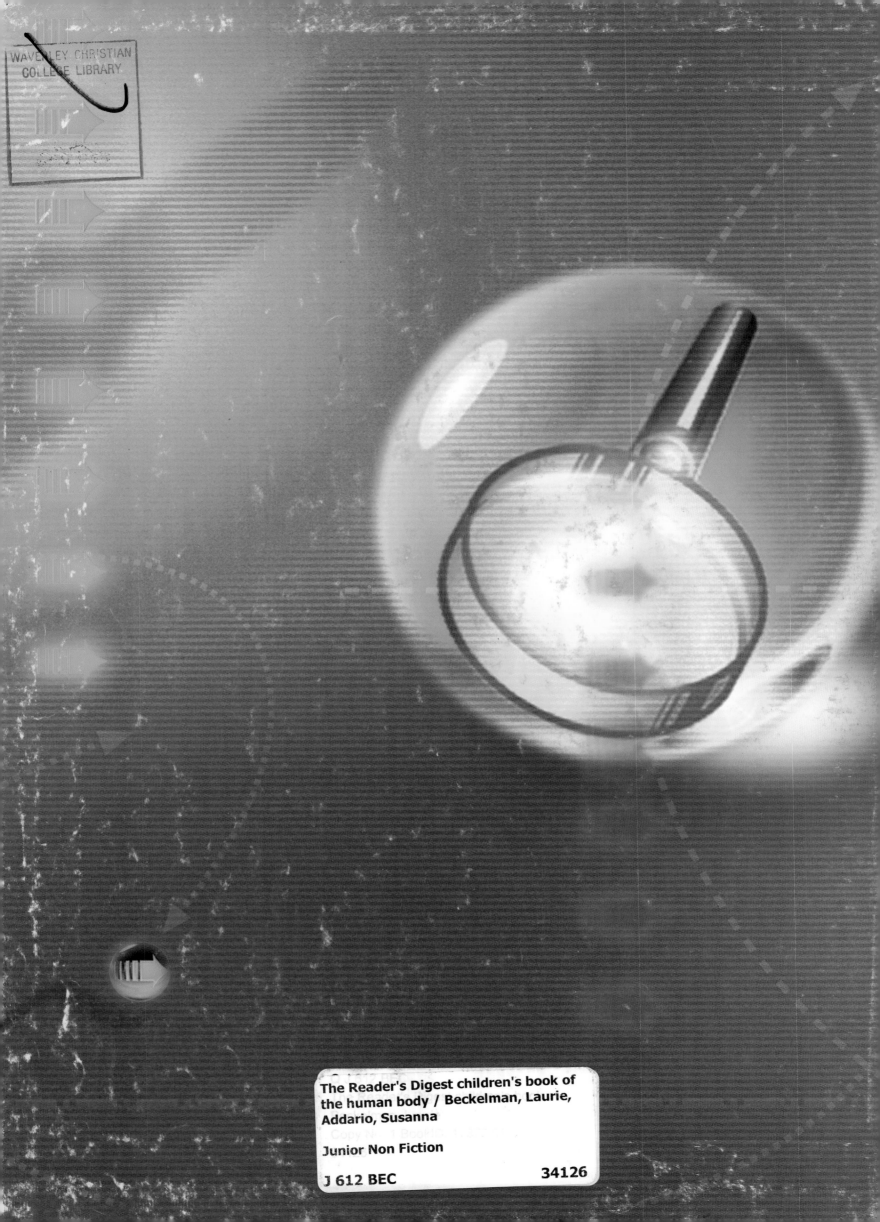